CONCILIUM

Religion in the Seventies

CONCILIUM

Concilium 125 (5/1979): Fundamental Theology

CHRISTIANITY AND THE BOURGEOISIE

Edited by
Johann Baptist Metz

THE SEABURY PRESS / NEW YORK

1979
The Seabury Press, 815 Second Avenue, New York, N.Y. 10017
ISBN: 0-8164-2233-8 (pbk.)   0-8164-0431-3

T. & T. Clark Ltd., 36 George Street, Edinburgh EH2 2LQ
ISBN: 0-567-30005-6 (pbk.)

Library of Congress Catalog Card Number: 79-65696
Printed in the United States of America

CONTENTS

Part III
Controversies

Editorial

A FUNDAMENTAL theology based on the premise that all theological statements have a practical basis is centrally concerned with the 'primacy of practice' and the search for the real subjects (bearers) of this practice. The 1978 volume looked for new situations and new subjects of theology. The purpose of this volume is to discuss the fundamental question of the religio-political practice of Christians, and to do so in such a way that the historical, social and economic conditions are neither obscured nor considered simply in the abstract. This work is necessary if Christianity is to be able to intervene in the worldwide conflicts which are today influencing the real fate of human beings and of the Churches. To this end the 1977 volume on 'Christianity and Socialism' is now followed by a volume which examines the relations of 'Christianity and the Bourgeoisie' (*Bürgertum*).

In this theological experiment the subjects which are missing or have had to be omitted are of particular importance (Christian and 'bourgeois' individuation, the 'bourgeois' principle of exchange and the Christian principle of solidarity, 'Christian values' in the constitutions of 'bourgeois' societies, etc.). Since some contributions arrived very late and could not be cut, what was originally planned as an extremely wide-ranging editorial was left extremely short of space. I must now present it with the hope that the volume, with the help of this outline of its structure, will be to some extent self-explanatory.

The volume first outlines the historical and political semantics of the terms 'bourgeois' and 'bourgeoisie' (Fetscher) and the sociological and theological issues raised by the discussion of class in religion (Baum, Fiorenza). There then follow essays on specific important theological aspects of the subject. Some attempt to show that there exists not just a Marxist, but also a Christian theological, critique of the 'bourgeois' world: from a biblical standpoint (Stegemann), through a discussion of Kierkegaard (Metz, with a contrary view from Løgstrup), Barth (Schellong), and Bonhoeffer (Gutierrez). Others discuss the relation of 'bourgeois' religion and popular religion in Christianity (Castillo), the loss of messianic religion in a 'bourgeois' Christianity (Metz), and elements of a theological critique of the '"bourgeois" world-view' (Schellong). There is an article on specific questions posed for 'bourgeois' societies by Jewish religious traditions (Waskow), and one on Christian elements of a non-'bourgeois' education (Beemer). Finally the volume deals with controversies over 'bourgeois' theologies and the theological justifications for replacing them (the authors' collective of van Leeuwen, van Dijk and Salemink), and with the legitimacy and the problems of non-'bourgeois' Christologies (Schiffers).

No wonder that in the rather unfamiliar subject-matter of this volume the conflict of theological opinions is reflected with particular clarity!

J. B. METZ

Translated by Francis McDonagh

Part I

General Orientations

Iring Fetscher

The 'Bourgeoisie' (*Bürgertum*, Middle Class): on the Historical and Political Semantics of the Term

THE ENGLISH *borough,* the Scots *burgh,* the French *bourg* and the German *Burg* derive from a Germanic word meaning fortified town. By the Middle High German period the principal meaning of *burc* was 'town'. *Burgher, bourgeois* and *Bürger* thus came to mean a town-dweller and, as towns developed political structures, a full member of the community. This origin gave *bourgeois* a dual meaning, a person following a trade in a town, an urban trader, etc. and a citizen, *polites,* a member of the political community.

While it is impossible here to go into the details of constitutional history, the role of this 'bourgeoisie' (*Bürgertum*) from the twelfth to the eighteenth centuries must be described at least in broad outline. The main influence on medieval society was rural feudalism. The cities generally developed under the protection of local magnates, who gradually rose to become a greater central power and freed themselves from the complex mutual obligations of the feudal system. This enabled the cities to develop in the German Empire—as 'Free Cities'—under the protection of the emperor, and later of the increasingly autonomous local princes. Through their tax yields they made a major contribution to the possibility of civil administration and princely state. The ideal type of this complex of factors can be seen in the rise of the bourgeoisie in France, which became the most important (material) support of the monarchy.

3

But great as was the independence from feudal society which the city dwellers won through their special development, the influence of the feudal hierarchy on the internal structures of the cities was no less great. The result was often the growth within the city community of quasi-orders of patricians, hierarchically organised guilds and so on, down to the day-wage labourers and escaped serfs, who, while they might be 'free' in the city ('City air brings freedom'), nonetheless never rose beyond the lowest step of the social pyramid. The expansion of trade and the growth of manufacture permitted a continual development of social and economic conditions in the cities in some areas of Europe, while—especially after the shift of trade routes to the oceans in the age of exploration—they stagnated in inland cities remote from the new lines of communication. Centres of city development and so also of 'bourgeois culture' included in turn the North Italian communes (Florence, Milan, Pisa, etc.), the Flemish and Dutch cities, finally those of England—with London by far the leader—and even earlier Paris, Lyons and Marseilles. For a time the bourgeoisie of the free German cities also prospered—in Nuremberg, Augsburg and so on—but the weakness of the territorial states (and the absence of a unified national state such as had developed in Spain, France and England) made this prosperity short-lived. The Reformation and the wars of religion later brought it to a complete decline.

For ideas and the prevailing terminology it is the development in France which has been the determining factor, probably down to the present. The victory of the French monarchy over the great feudal lords was largely due to the support of the bourgeoisie. At the same time the *noblesse de robe,* the nobility of office newly created by the king who served the country as officials, judges and officers, was a substitute for the bourgeoisie, though it was largely its sons who acquired these newly created positions. Within the framework of the unified national territorial state trade and manufacture could develop faster, as could the bourgeoisie, and in particular the upper stratum of the bourgeoisie. Still formally a part of the 'Third Estate' until the French Revolution, the prosperous upper bourgeoisie began to feel the traditional hierarchical society with its legal restrictions (for example on the free movement of labour and landed property) as an irksome fetter. The struggle between the rising bourgeoisie and the feudal aristocracy, which hitherto had been waged almost with the help of the monarchy and the bureaucracy it had created, sharpened, especially when influential groups among the old aristocracy obstructed further reform of the state in the interests of the upper bourgeoisie (fall of finance minister Necker, etc.). With hindsight the French Revolution can be seen as a revolution of the upper bourgeoisie, though this group could be sure of the support of the other sectors of the 'Third Estate'. The whole feudal pyramid of orders was abolished and the formal legal equality of all Frenchmen (*as citoyens*) established.

It is only at this point, after the revolutionary abolition of the old hierarchical society, that an entity describable as a 'bourgeois class' exists—or begins to form. Until this point, strictly speaking, there existed only an upper bourgeois stratum within the Third Estate. Societies are organised into orders when different sections of the population have different legal status (serfdom, vassalage, freedom, etc.). A class society is characterised by the fact that individuals are members of particular social groups (classes), as a result, not of legal, but simply of economic differences in their situations. It is nevertheless true that the bourgeoisie developed as a class within the framework of the old hierarchical society. It developed specific attitudes, its own culture, its own value system and particular varieties of religion (Protestantism, Calvinism, Jansenism, etc.), varieties, moreover, which, despite all national differences, nevertheless show—within Europe at least—certain common features.

It is really only Marxism which has developed a precise definition of the bourgeoisie, and this definition will therefore be used in the rest of this article as the basis for a phenomenological description and analysis. For Marx a 'bourgeois' is a capitalist, i.e., a person who, by virtue of ownership of means of production on a considerable scale, lives off the organisation and exploitation of the labour power of others and manages his resources in a capitalistic way. A precise figure for the minimum value of means of production owned which makes a person a capitalist (a 'bourgeois') cannot be given, since this figure changes in the course of the development of industrial capitalism. The crucial feature is that the capitalist no longer has to work in his own enterprise and usually (in classical capitalism) limits himself to the organisation of production and sale, whereas in fully developed and late capitalism he abandons even these functions to paid managers and lives entirely on the interest from the capital. More important than the amount of capital which differentiates a capitalist from a member of the 'middle class', from the small commodity producer who produces things with his own means of production, but also—to some extent at least—with his own labour power, is the capitalist mode of production. To the advocates of this new economic system—the French Physiocrats (Quesnay, Turgot, Dupont de Nemours, etc.) and Adam Smith—this method seemed the only rational and 'natural' one. Capitalist economic activity means reinvesting at least a considerable part of the surplus (surplus value) produced, i.e., constantly expanding one's business. 'Accumulate, accumulate, that is the Law and the Prophets', as Marx once glossed the 'profession of the capitalist'. In England as early as the sixteenth century large landowners operated in this way: they abandoned the traditional economy, in which the main aims were the provision of necessities and the prestige which came from the largest possible number of peasants and servants, and they increased yields—for example by turning arable land into pasture—and also to some extent invested surpluses in the City of London. The inhuman consequences of this 'rational husbandry' were attacked at the time by Thomas More in his *Utopia*. In Marx's thought, then, 'bourgeois' equals capitalist, but there have been and are very many members of other social strata who also think of themselves as 'bourgeois'. If Marx's definition is strictly applied, the 'bourgeoisie' form no more than a tiny minority in present highly industrialised societies. It is true that we must include in the 'bourgeoisie', a large number of top managers with high incomes (part of which is paid in shares of the firms concerned), but even so this class as a whole would probably make up little more than 1 per cent of the population.

If we continue for the moment with a 'functional' distinction of social groups, the 'true bourgeoisie' (the capitalist class) is followed in the social pyramid by the 'commercial middle class', including shopkeepers and so on. This group, whose economic importance has declined heavily as a result of the developments of the last hundred years, still makes up a considerable proportion of the population. It must be taken as including all those owners of means of production who work in their own businesses (as artisans or traders, etc.) and/or employ so few staff that they cannot attain much more than a petty bourgeois standard of living. It is obvious that the distinction here is not simple, and it is probably necessary to postulate an intermediate level of 'small capitalists' in between the commercial middle class and the upper 'bourgeoisie'.

However, even those groups within highly industrialised societies who do not possess their own means of production (the 'classical' sign of the 'bourgeoisie'), but live off a wage or salary, cannot be included *en masse* in the 'proletariat'. A distinction has to be made here between highly paid white-collar workers (mostly with university degrees) and senior and top civil servants on the one hand and the mass of white-collar workers on the other, who in standard of living and level of income do not differ in any noticeable way from industrial workers, and indeed often have lower incomes.

Here again, the distinction within the higher paid groups is not totally simple. Attempts have been made, for example to distinguish senior staff from others on the ground that they have authority to hire and fire other staff independently. However, in addition to this still functional distinction, income level, life-style, level of education and the individual's assessment of himself are usually the determining factors. In so far as white-collar workers are not top managers and so part of the upper 'bourgeoisie', they form an intermediate stratum which has also been labelled 'the new petty bourgeoisie'.

Officials, especially higher officials in the administration, judiciary and so on, were traditionally linked with the 'bourgeoisie' (at least on the Continent in contrast to the development in Great Britain and the USA). They came mainly from 'bourgeois' or 'petty bourgeois' groups, shared their national ideology and were only partly differentiated from them by their attitude to the 'bureaucracy'. Moreover, the attitude of the 'true bourgeoisie' to the state bureaucracy changed fundamentally many times in the course of history. Before the French Revolution the state bureaucracy and the rising propertied 'bourgeoisie' were allies in the struggle against the old nobility and its privileges. After the Revolution large sections of the 'bourgeoisie' came to feel the bureaucracy as a brake. In the period of liberal competitive capitalism, at least, there were repeated conflicts and disputes. In the period of imperialism, when the state bureaucracy and the armed forces became important instruments of economic policy in the interests of the upper 'bourgeoisie', there was again a large measure of agreement. With the creation of the welfare state, however, this attitude has changed again, and the 'state bureaucracy' is again increasingly criticised in so far as it intervenes to help weaker members of society. There is, of course, no such criticism when the state machine distributes subsidies to business.

Finally, there is the special position of the so-called 'bourgeois intelligentsia'. By this term I mean—again primarily with reference to the Continent of Europe—the stratum of writers, artists, journalists and so on who, while through their education they can be said to share in the 'bourgeois inheritance', nevertheless, as a result of the precariousness of their economic positions, usually adopt an extremely ambivalent attitude towards the 'bourgeoisie'. These groups produce the bitterest critics of the bourgeoisies (see the caricatures of George Gross) and its outlook. The 'bourgeois' becomes the symbol of philistinism, egoism, rigidity, narrowness, and so on. This polemic against the 'bourgeoisie', with its strong aesthetic and moral undertone, must be distinguished from the political struggle waged against the 'bourgeoisie' (capitalism) by socialist movements (proletarian militants in the class struggle), though in the literary reflection of these struggles the two types of polemic often intertwine. The distinction is necessary for an understanding, for example, of the contempt shown by intellectuals (many intellectuals) for workers who 'have become bourgeois', a contempt which often far exceeds in bitterness their contempt for the 'bourgeoisie' itself.

In the day-to-day political battle an attempt is often made—especially by conservatives—to replace a differentiated, objective concept of the 'bourgeoisie' by a cliché which enables as many people as possible to identify with it. The very term 'middle class', which in Great Britain still has meaning as a result of the existence of an old aristocracy (albeit one no longer economically dominant), has on the Continent a mystifying function. The third edition of the German 'Handbook of Politics', published in 1930, contained the following passage: 'The German bourgeoisie (*Bürgertum*), i.e., all the members of the German national community who regard the freedom of the individual and the maintenance and cultivation of national consciousness as the main foundations for the security of the necessary external conditions of life, is today engaged in a battle with Marxism.' (Here a political position and acceptance of a particular ideology (nationalism and individualism) are made a criterion of class membership. The class is, as it were, opened wide so that as many people as possible can identify with it. For this purpose particular ideological elements belonging to 'bourgeois' culture (here individualism and nationalism) are put on display to create the impression that they are the essential. Alfred Meusel, in the article on the 'bourgeoisie' (*Bürgertum*) in the *Handwörterbuch für Soziologie* (ed. Alfred Vierkandt, Stuttgart 1931), quotes the *Deutsche Bergwerkszeitung* (No 82, vol. 31, 1930), in which the political motives for such a broad interpretation of the term are very plainly stated: 'Only then will business be able to mobilise the masses of all the little people who fear for their possessions, which may be few but have been painfully acquired and are so all the more tenaciously defended [i.e. if it succeeds in mobilising the 'middle class' (*Mittelstond*)]. Without this sort of backing, indeed without a majority, nothing can be done, especially in the age of democracy and parliamentarism. When the big man comes to the aid of the little man in the battle against annihilating Marxism, the little man will be grateful to him and, above all, he will vote the right way.' The polemical reference to Marxism (which is also here a code word for all the working-class parties) also has an inherent justification in so far as it is the objective class concept of Marxism which is the main obstacle to the aim of creating a 'national community' of upper, petty and lower 'bourgeoisie' (the 'embourgeoised' proletariat). Just as the concept of the 'bourgeoisie' is turned into an ideological attitude, 'proletariat' is also turned into an 'attitudinal concept'. The one is emotionally inflated, the other similarly deflated. The total success of these endeavours can be seen in retrospect in the results of surveys of people's own assessment of their class status. Fewer and fewer class themselves as 'proletarians'.

Another favourite argument used by conservative politicians to obscure social realities is the claim that class conflicts are not an objective fact, but a product of 'Marxist agitation' among the workers, and would not exist at all without Marxism.

It is not just specific facts of social history or sociology which are associated with the 'bourgeoisie', however, but also a whole range of cultural phenomena. The rise of the 'bourgeoisie' is accompanied by: the triumph of the modern sciences and technology, the individualistic calculation of utility as the basic rule of life, the legitimation of individual love as the basis of communal life, the rejection of any non-democratic foundation for state power, a high regard for work, industry and thrift as typical 'bourgeois' virtues (to which cleanliness and tidiness are subsequently added). The final stage is the secularisation of basic philosophies (from revealed religion to 'manifest' religion, (Hegel), from theism to deism, from fideism to agnosticism) and the glorification of the nation (patriotism and nationalism), attitudes which were all unknown to the traditional aristocracy and the middle ages (or made an appearance only as exceptional phenomena).

1 *Individualism;* As relations between people cease to be fixed by class membership, and individual behaviour ceases to be determined by traditional norms (even down to prescribed dress), the tradition is replaced as the source of happiness (and unhappiness) by the *anonymous market.* In the ideal society composed entirely of independent commodity producers the relations of all to each other are determined solely by the objective laws of the market operating behind the backs of the individuals. The formation of the individual is also a result of the formation of market relations as the dominant form of social relations. It is only now, with the rise of 'bourgeois' trade, industry and application to work that artists begin to sign their works. The individual sculptor or painter now no longer feels himself a member of a wider community such as a workshop, but a unique individual. He sees his work as an expression of this personality and also wants it attributed to him. At the same time he develops into a producer of 'branded goods' ('Rubenses') and so—in some cases—comes close to the type of the capitalist entrepreneur. Relations between the sexes become freed from pre-existing and prescribed norms. Subjective sexual love becomes the only legitimate (and the essential) condition for a union. In *Romeo and Juliet* Shakespeare vividly portrayed this breaking away of individual love from the prescriptions of the clan. The clash between class morality and individual love continued to be a favourite subject of the 'bourgeois' novel and 'bourgeois' tragedy until well into the nineteenth century. It is no accident that the young Napoleon (a parvenu from a background in the lower aristocracy and 'bourgeoisie') was enthusiastic for Goethe's Werther, that advocate of spontaneous, subjective sexual love in the face of convention and the establishment. On the other hand, this approach ignores the fact that for a large part of the population such 'individualism' remains an unattainable luxury. Only a person who is economically free can follow his heart. The beauty of a girl from a proletarian family is 'available' to the prosperous

man about town, but not to his poor colleague. The other side of individualism is often enough egoism and cold calculation. 'Every man for himself—and God for all', runs the well-known slogan. Nevertheless individualism certainly ranks as one of the great achievements of the 'bourgeoisie'. Only at this stage—and, without any exaggeration, only in a relatively short period of its history—did the 'bourgeoisie' make possible individual freedom and the free development of individual character, though only for a minority.

2. *Utilitarianism:* The only behaviour regarded by the 'bourgeoisie' as rational is that which calculates individual utility (the maximisation of utility) rationally and makes the result of this calculation the basis of practical activity. As early as the beginning of the eighteenth century Bernard de Mandeville, in his *Fable of the Bees,* illustrated the theory, later taken up by Adam Smith, that in a market society 'private vices' lead to 'public profit'. In other words, out of the combination and opposition of utilitarian (egoistical) calculations there emerges, as it were, the social optimum. Apart from the economic criticism which can be brought against this liberal model, it naturally also had moral consequences. An increasingly large discrepancy developed between Christian virtues and patterns of behaviour—which continued to be taught—on the one hand and the attitudes regarded by the new economic system as the only 'rational' ones on the other. Rousseau at an early stage identified the separation of 'being and seeming' as the most important characteristic of the new age. Hidden behind the utilitarianism and egoism as the legitimating ideology is the assumption that differences in success in life are an expression or consequence of differences in 'performance' or even a reward for services to the community. For the Calvinist or the Puritan this mythology may be replaced by the explanation of one's own economic success as a result of God's unfathomable gracious election. If economic success is regarded as a sign of gracious election, failure must also be regarded as an indicator of reprobation.

3. *Industry as a new virtue. The morality of work:* Industry appears for the first time as an important virtue in the work of Arnold Geulincx—in the seventeenth century. Classical philosophy could not see industry as a particular human virtue (*arété*). According to Aristotle, who was followed by scholastic philosophy, human activities were the more valuable the more they found their meaning and purpose within themselves. Industry, however, is only a mode of work, of producing, and so can only be 'valuable' when measured by the goal which the effort serves. It is a typically secondary virtue raised by the 'bourgeoisie' to the rank of a supreme value. Aristotle's principle is that 'we are unleisured in order to be at leisure'. For the monastic orders prayer (and meditation) always retained equal status alongside work, but for the bourgeois utilitarianism

of the eighteenth century, leisure, contemplation and prayer—the *vita contemplativa*—lost all value. Voltaire attacks the hundreds of thousands of 'idle monks, nuns and priests' in France. In the unfavourable comparison of the prosperity of Catholic and Protestant states the lack of enthusiasm for work in the former and the higher number of Catholic holidays is cited disapprovingly as one of the causes. Industry and work in the sense of productive activity turns from a necessary means (to which human beings are 'condemned') to being an end in itself. The point of life is not a life of leisure or the development of capacities for artistic, meditative or philosophical activity, but the accumulation of wealth, to which diligent work is a means. These two views, work as an end in itself and work as a means to accumulating wealth, are two poles between which 'bourgeois' ideas swing. What raises effort to its highest value, however, is the interpretation of earthly success (affluence, prosperity), as in Calvinism, as a sign confirming the divine gracious election, which makes it highly desirable.

4. *Rationality and instrumental reason:* The rising 'bourgeoisie's' battle against traditional feudal society and its culture takes place under the banner of reason. At first this is taken to mean both individual, subjective rationality and the objective rationality of a better social and political order. This social and political order is supposed to correspond to an *ordre naturel* now at last discovered by the economic sciences (Physiocrats, Smith). The political order, based on the equality of all men, is to rest on the voluntary agreement of the citizens. Both views of the objectively rational order were corrected in the course of time and gave way to an 'instrumental reason' which in the end was the only position defended. The socio-economic order—as Adam Smith can already see quite clearly—involves considerable disadvantages for the majority of propertyless wage-earners, who have to rely on an increasingly unrealistic hope of individual betterment. The political order of democracy is based on the assumption that every citizen will also be an independent bourgeois employing his own means of production. The result was that an increasing number of people were theoretically excluded from full citizenship. In the French Constitution of 1791 messengers and wage-labourers (journeymen) are explicitly excluded from the passive franchise (the right to be elected). Other countries had a franchise based on a property qualification, which favoured the owners of great fortunes: in Prussia until 1918 there was a three-class voting system which gave the upper two tax groups, which comprised only a small percentage of the population, as many votes each as the third. The demand for the establishment of an 'objectively rational order' thus became a threat for defenders of the *status quo*. The concept of objective reason receded and was finally rejected completely. What is rational now became what was

rational in terms of a specific purpose, the choice of suitable means to ends about which no critical questions were asked. The goal as it were 'demanded' by the socio-economic system was now economic growth, the expansion of reproduction, and the means to this goal was instrumental reason. The possibility that the inexorable goals could make the system itself irrational was simply denied. Another source of purposes for the economic system was the scientifically based technology of the conquest of nature.

In creating the capitalist mode of production, the unified state and the world market, the 'bourgeoisie' has given an enormous impetus to historical development. It was the first really 'revolutionary' class. It radically transformed the mode of production in a few centuries, from one based on peasant craftsmen via manufacture to industrial production. From the harnessing of water and steam power via electricity to atomic energy, it tapped enormous sources of energy and increased the productivity of human labour several hundredfold. This made it possible also to multiply the amount of commodities while at the same time shortening labour time.

However, the problems associated with this process were visible almost from the beginning, and they have today reached such dimensions that no one can any longer ignore them. Individualism and utilitarianism ('every man for himself') have cooled human relations to such an extent that many people are suffering from this to the point of mental illness. The exploitation of nature and the unplanned transformation of unspoilt countryside into roads, airports, factories and so on has begun to threaten the natural basis of human existence. The uneven development among the industrial nations, and even more between the industrial states and the Third World, is leading to political tensions and making political interventions in the 'automatic' process unavoidable. The working-class movement and the movements which, after the political liberation of the former colonies, now seek their economic independence, have as their aims a total revision of the results of bourgeois-capitalist development.

At the same time the values and norms of the 'bourgeoisie' are being threatened by growing sections of the 'bourgeoisie', the 'petty bourgeoisie' and the workers whose class ties have been weakened. Diligence and industry can be accepted less and less as ends in themselves. Economic growth which threatens the bases of life is no longer accepted without qualification as 'progress'. A rationality limited to instrumental reason is increasingly coming to seem inadequate. Critical rethinking about the behavioural pressures produced by the structure of the socio-economic system is being increasingly demanded. In this process the critique is going beyond the framework of the older critique of capitalism as formulated most clearly by Marxism. Marx's other fundamental charge against the capitalist economy was that its dynamic would fail before reaching a level of production sufficient to meet all real needs. We know today that there is nothing wrong with this dynamic, but the direction of the process gives rise to increasing anxiety. What is now required is not a continuation and increase of the quantitative growth of industrial production, but a critical appraisal of its direction and a revision of the mode of production's own immanent goals. This is why many critics today regard the goals of the bureaucratic planners in the countries of 'real socialism' as 'state capitalist' because they do not seek a model for an alternative way of living, but simply to 'catch up and overtake' the productive capacity of the capitalist industrial countries. Such a model of an alternative way of living presupposes changes in many 'bourgeois' values and attitudes. The main thing will be to bring about this change without sacrificing too many human values and yet within the relatively short time mankind has available if it is to avoid total ecological devastation. The most important parts of the inheritance of the 'bourgeois' period to be preserved are therefore individual freedom and the use of reason as a criterion. These must remain the two binding principles, freedom in the sense of the right of all individuals to full development of their unique individuality, and reason in the sense of a way of life and mode of production based on rational goals which are open to inspection by all in a free discussion. Because of the crisis of capitalist and 'bourgeois' industrial civilisation there is a great danger that even these essential aspects of the 'bourgeois' inheritance will be rejected. I see in the growing popularity of exotic cults and irrational creeds (astrology, cheiromancy, miraculous healing, etc.), and in the tendency to equate the value of science on the one hand and shamanism and so on on the other (as recommended by Paul Feyerabend), signs of such a total rejection of bourgeois culture, in which even the achievements of the bourgeois period are in danger of being lost.

Almost the whole age of the 'bourgeoisie' is characterised by a striking swing to and fro between a euphoric belief in progress and an expectation of collapse, moods which seem to run parallel to political and economic events. At the beginning of the process we had a romantic adulation of unspoilt nature. Most recently an uncritical exaggeration of the possibility of unlimited progress brought us the long period of prosperity in the industrial nations after the Second World War. However, since technical resources have reached the point where they allow worldwide collective suicide many times over and the results of industrial growth can be predicted with at least relative precision, human beings have been forced to turn from fits of hope or despair to responsible planning for their fate. What is theoretically possible and necessary can nevertheless be carried out in political reality only with great effort. To this process science can contribute only relentless intellectual effort and education. If the human race is not to be dragged into the collapse of the 'bourgeoisie', it must shake off the influence of 'bourgeois' capitalist industrial civilisation, but without thereby abandoning its valuable achievements.

Translated by Francis McDonagh

Gregory Baum

Middle Class Religion
in America

KARL MARX, in his *Theories of Surplus Value*, speaks of 'the constantly growing number of the middle classes, those who stand between the workman on the one hand and the capitalist and landlord on the other'. These middle classes, Marx declares, 'are a burden weighing heavily on the working base and increase the social security and the power of the upper ten thousand'.[1] This remarkable statement, clear-sighted though it be, does not fit well into the theoretical framework of Marx's own sociology. Normally he contends that the people in the middle, whom he usually calls 'petty bourgeoisie', will have diminishing significance in the class structure of capitalist societies.

Marx's intuition was prophetic. The number of propertyless, non-manual (white-collar) workers has enormously increased in modern capitalist societies, nowhere as much as in the United States of America. According to some estimates white-collar and blue-collar workers are of equal strength in the USA, a proportion that has been reached by no other country. It has also been observed that in the USA a growing overlap or merger is taking place between white-collar and blue-collar workers. Through collective bargaining a considerable section of the manual workers has achieved higher wages and social security, equivalent to the standards of many white-collar workers. Pension funds and various insurance schemes provided for organised labour often creates an economic outlook among workers that resembles the middle class. At the same time white-collar workers themselves have in many instances been unionised and by engaging in collective bargaining have acquired a consciousness that resembles manual workers. Finally it has been argued that

15

changes have taken place at the work place itself that in many instances obliterate the difference between manual and non-manual labour. For automation in the factory may transform manual labour into the handling of buttons and switches, while the computer and other speed-up technology in the office often makes clerks and sales people into machine operators. Because of these trends, it has been argued, the workers in America have become middle class. Through their work and employment the vast majority of people see themselves as belonging to the same class. They acknowledge a small minority of the very rich at the top, the owning and managing elite, and a minority at the bottom, the under-class, the destitute and unemployable, who are forever locked into their poverty. This middle class is of course divided by levels of power and prestige, but it is possible through hard work and achievement to climb the ladder of success or at least to see one's children move to a higher status. It has been argued that this extraordinary social mobility is the reason, or at least one of the reasons, why the United States of America, alone among the Western nations, has never produced a nationwide socialist movement nor a working class political party. Some sociologists argue that since the middle class represents the vast majority, America has become in its own way a classless society.[2] Robert Nisbet, the distinguished conservative sociologist, writes 'today, as a sociological concept, class is dead'.[3]

1. MIDDLE CLASS IDEOLOGY

The theory of America as the middle class society or even the classless society is an enormous exaggeration of existing trends. The trends mentioned in the above paragraph do exist, but they affect only sections of the white- and blue-collar workers; they do not constitute a shift in the whole of society. There can be no doubt that capitalism in any of its forms creates classes: it is inevitable that in capitalism people share the same fate, the same conditions, the same possibilities depending on their relation to the market, even though the level of class structuration may vary from country to country.

The theory of middle class America diverts attention from those sections of society that do not fit the total picture. It makes invisible the unchallenged power of the men at the top, the owners and managers of the large-scale corporations, on whose decisions the rest of the population depends. In times of economic crisis in particular, the people are made to feel their social impotence, whether they be small businessmen and producers (the old middle class), white-collar workers (the new middle class) or manual labourers. The theory makes invisible a large section of the working class that suffers grave economic hardship and perpetual insecurity. It diverts attention altogether from the part of America that has been structured into poverty, 'the other America' as it has been called.[4] It makes invisible the racial minorities that experience discrimination and are imprisoned in powerlessness. It has sometimes been argued that the manual workers of America form a dual labour force, one that is organised and has achieved some security, made up mainly of white males, and the other non-organised, insecure, made up mainly of women and racial minorities. The theory of middle class America also disguises the regional disparities in America, the exploitative relationship between metropolis and hinterland, and the existence of sections of the population, including white Anglo-Saxons, which have been caught in long lasting destitution.[5] Finally, the theory makes invisible the relation of American affluence to the economy of the rest of the world, in particular Latin America.

The class structure of America deserves careful analysis. It is a mistake to think of 'class' simply as economic stratification and to define, as some sociologists do, the lower, middle and upper classes in terms of annual income, without paying attention to their relation to production. At the same time it is a mistake to approach American society with previously defined categories, such as 'bourgeoisie' and 'proletariat', which do not shed light on the class structure of America. It is worth mentioning in this issue of *Concilium* that 'bourgeois' is not an English word: to know what it means people consult a dictionary. It does not carry the technical meaning as the owners of the productive machinery, it does not refer to the one time revolutionary class that sought to dismantle the feudal order. In dictionaries, 'bourgeois' is vaguely rendered as 'middle class'; the word is usually used, we are told, to refer to the highly conventional taste and style adopted by certain middle class people. To the English-speaking public it sounds strange to hear farmers and fishermen referred to as 'petty bourgeois' because they own their own tools of production. The use of 'bourgeoisie' and 'proletariat', so readily employed in Marxist literature, easily gives the impression to North Americans that a ready-made social theory, tailored in the nineteenth-century Europe, is imposed upon modern society in America. Incidentally, British and Canadian socialism have always avoided these words. Their spokesmen wanted to show that bearers of socialism are several groups—workers, farmers, minorities of various kinds. While ignoring Gramsci's concept 'the historic bloc', British and Canadian socialism tried to find a language that would unite the various groups that suffer systematic exclusion and exploitation in the existing capitalist society.

While the term 'middle class' in a technical sense refers to the propertyless, non-manual workers, i.e. the salaried in business, industry, government and education (the new middle class) and includes the owners of small businesses and the independent professions (the old middle class), it is useful to employ the term 'middle class' in symbolic fashion as referring to all those people who regard themselves as middle class.

The theory of America as a middle class society does not stand up. Still, it corresponds to the image which many Americans have of their own social world. They regard themselves as middle class set in a middle class society and hence believe they are not identified with any class at all. This image of society, mediated by mainstream culture, serves people as the key for estimating their life chances and future possibilities and interpreting the inequalities, conflicts and troubles in their own nation. The theory of America as a middle class society turns out to be a powerful ideology, an image that distorts the perception of society for the sake of assuring its stability.

What are some of the elements of this middle class ideology? This article is not the place to pursue this issue in great detail. Let me mention only four elements, some of which have already been named. (1) There is first of all the idea that the vast majority of Americans enjoy equality of opportunity. American society is such that those who work hard, apply themselves and make use of their talents can succeed. Human life is here seen in highly individualistic terms: each person is called upon to promote his or her own career. (2) Connected with this is the idea that those who do not achieve security and well-being have only themselves to blame: they did not try hard enough. This idea is sometimes applied to explain the presence of the poor, the misfits, the unsuccessful; but it is more often applied by people against themselves. The ideology leads people to despise themselves if they are failures; lack of success makes them feel guilty and unworthy. (3) The middle class ideology, as has been pointed out, makes the racial minorities invisible. It becomes possible to generalise about American life without adverting to the large number of minority groups who are caught in socio-economic traps that prevent them from 'making it'. It also leaves wholly unreflected the real impact of the power elite on the day-to-day conditions of life. When something goes wrong in society, people must struggle to rectify it and if necessary, ask the government for assistance, but the economic system itself is never questioned. Capitalism is simply the American system and to find fault with it is a failure of national sentiment. (4) Middle class ideology, finally, takes for granted the universal consensus in American society. Since the middle class regards itself as identical with the people, it applies its standards to the whole of the population. The language of unity, reconciliation and consensus hides the attempt to negate the existing conflicts and the inequality of power and promotes a self-understanding of the nation in which even the marginalised see themselves as part of the upwardly mobile crowd.

2. MIDDLE CLASS RELIGION

We now turn to the question raised in this issue of *Concilium*. Is there a middle class religion in America? Every society in this fallen world is sinful, i.e. has built into it injustices or social mechanisms that push some people into deprivation and diminish their life chances. (Since this is true of all societies, voluntary or natural, it also applies to the Churches.) Mainstream culture, I wish to argue, tries to make these injustices invisible. Since the dominant culture is promoted by the powerful in society and meant to legitimate the inherited order, it tends to close people's eyes to the existing contradictions. This distorting process affects secular as well as religious culture. Already the prophets of Israel revealed to the people that they used their religion to blind themselves in regard to the true nature of their society, Jesus himself made known the hidden injuries inflicted upon the ordinary people by the dominant religious culture and its link to political authority. Religion is subject to ideological distortion. We cannot avoid the question, therefore, whether and to what extent American Christianity has become a middle class religion.

The question calls to mind Will Herberg's influential sociological study, *Protestant, Catholic, Jew*, published in 1955, which demonstrated that the Churches and synagogues of America while differing among themselves in regard to doctrine and organisation, in fact promoted the same ideals, the identical ethos, the same moral vision, namely 'the American way of life'.[6] This analysis was confirmed by Protestant theologians in the late 'fifties.[7] In the 'sixties, sociologists, following Robert Bellah, began to speak of the civil religion of America.[8] The political vision of America's historical destiny, it was argued, has profoundly affected the self-symbolisation of the entire nation and influenced, in largely unconscious manner, the historic religions, Christian and Jewish. It should be noted, however, that in the ensuing controversy 'civil religion' was understood in quite different ways: some social scientists understood it as the religious legitimation of the existing order of America and its aggressive foreign policy, while others regarded it as a set of transcendent norms in the light of which Americans evaluate the domestic and external policies of their nation. According to the latter, the youth movement's condemnation of institutional racism at home and economic and military imperialism abroad, was an exercise of civil religion.

These are generalisations. When we study American religion in detail we find many counter-currents. Since Catholics were on the whole the later immigrants in America who expected equality yet experienced bigotry and discrimination, popular Catholic religion must be analysed by taking into consideration the elements of resistance and self-affirmation which the various ethnic groups expressed through their faith. The Catholic Church helped the people to move from the folk culture of their own background to the urban culture of their new setting and at the same time protected their collective identity in a Protestant land. Catholic piety helped the immigrants to join the mainstream economically while remaining culturally apart. At the end of the nineteenth century and the beginning of the twentieth, Catholics made up over half of the work force in America, which meant on the one hand that the Catholic hierarchy acknowledged the labour movement and defended trade unions and collective bargaining (even prior to Leo XIII's *Rerum Novarum*) at a time when the Protestant Churches, the government, and local authorities still opposed them; it meant on the other hand that the labour movement, especially the American Federation of Labour, was imbued with a strong anti-socialist character.[9] Of course, there were also Protestant ethnic groups who went through the immigrant experience. Then there was the vast sector of English-speaking, Protestant poor whose religion also contained elements of resistance and confrontation. The same was true in a more startling manner of black religion. Any hasty generalisation of American religion is, therefore, quite impossible.

Still, it is possible and in fact necessary to point to the trends of middle class religion in America, leaving open the question to what extent these trends are actually found in the various churches. 'Political theology' regards it as its major task to uncover the ideological nature of mainstream Christianity and then to formulate the Christian message in a manner that negates and transcends the manifestations of middle class religion.[10] Middle class religion, if I may repeat, is part of mainstream culture and hence exercises a very similar function. Recalling the characterisations of mainstream culture, I wish to describe in the briefest of terms its religious and theological equivalents.

Middle class individualism has its spiritual counterpart: the emphasis on personal salvation. Here Jesus is seen as the saviour who rescues us one by one from the catastrophe of history. Through faith, a person is related to God, is healed, restored, brought into holiness and saved for eternal life. This approach can lead to such a concentration of the individual that life after death becomes the entire religious preoccupation. Earthly life is here a testing ground where individuals demonstrate their fidelity to God and then graduate to the realm of heaven. Man's historical existence and mission are here wholly relativised. While such a view of grace and salvation is basically at odds with the genius of Catholicism, there are signs that such ideas pervade even Catholic piety.

Related to this is the second point: the need to blame oneself for failures. In religion this trend shapes a particular view of sin and guilt. God becomes here the great accuser. We are presented with rules and high ideals and asked to do well and move forward. If we live up to the divine expectation, we are rewarded; but if we fail, we live in guilt waiting for the divine punishment. There is no awareness here that the order in which we live is sinful and that the injustices built into society damage us and disable us, and that therefore failure in our personal lives is a symptom of the world's sin. The highly private notion of sin exempts the institutions from critical examination. In this piety what counts is to try hard. And if we fail to try hard, then we are no good, then we are guilty and hate ourselves.

As mainstream culture makes invisible the underprivileged minorities, so does middle class religion. American religion creates denominational loyalties. People are engaged with their own co-religionists in the struggle for economic well-being in a society that is owned and ruled by 'others'. Catholics even felt that they were not wholly welcome in America. Since the focus is here on the struggle of one's own group, there was little awareness of the wholly disadvantaged people in society. The marginals became easily invisible. Institutional racism, the systematic discrimination of the non-white peoples, did not—until recently—emerge as a major issue in religious consciousness. Even though the percentage of Spanish-speaking minorities is high in the Catholic Church, some suggest as high as 20 per cent, the ordinary Catholic is not aware of this: Mexican Americans and Puerto Ricans are not present in the self-understanding of the Catholic community.

Middle class piety overlooks the enormous social gaps between people and believes that the Christian message has the same meaning for all, beyond the differences of class. Sermons and spiritual counsels are given as if all belonged to the mythical middle class. To respond to world hunger a preacher will ask people to opt for a more modest life and a simpler diet without any awareness that some families in the congregation are unable to feed their children properly. Church leaders use the word 'materialistic' in a pejorative sense as if they are thinking of the well-to-do who long for a sail boat or a house in the country; if they thought of parents who long for money so that their children can have their teeth cared for or get a better education, churchmen would not use pejorative language to describe the desire for greater income.

Finally, middle class religion easily speaks of unity and reconciliation. It disguises the real conflicts in the community and the inequality of power and pretends that love can unite all people in a common humanity. Middle class religion entertains the hope that the great injustices in the world, including the gap between rich nations and poor nations, can be overcome through greater love: if all people became more generous, helped and forgave one another and co-operated in the building of the one world, the world's problems could be overcome.

3. THE TRANSCENDENCE OF THE GOSPEL

In the 'sixties, middle class ideology in America was seriously challenged. The noise made by the discriminated and the protest of the youth movement against the ethos and the underlying political thrust of the middle classes created a new self-perception among many Americans. This had a strong echo in the churches. A network of Christians all over the continent tried to demonstrate the transcendence of the Gospel over middle class religion, and they did so by action, life style, a new spirituality, and a critical theology.

To illustrate this affirmation of transcendence let me refer to a single document, the pastoral letter, *From Words to Action*, published by the Canadian bishops in 1976. (While many of the social, political and economic problems of Canada differ from those of the United States, the presence of middle class religion in Canada is powerful indeed.) The Canadian bishops begin the pastoral letter with a critique of capitalism. They reject the present economic system because it widens the gap between the rich and the poor, especially between rich nations and poor nations, and because it places the control of resources in the hands of a small minority. Capitalism fails to meet the human needs of the majority of people. Christians are called upon to struggle for a more just social order. This is not an optional activity, it is integral to bringing the Gospel to the world. The bishops admit that until now only 'a minority' of Catholics are following this path, but they regard them as a 'significant minority' since they challenged the entire Church to greater fidelity. This minority, the bishops say, has often been misunderstood and criticised, 'especially by the more affluent and powerful sectors of their communities'. The bishops acknowledge class conflict in the Church. The more affluent and powerful sectors in the community want to protect middle class religion. We cannot take refuge, the bishops continue, in the position that our duty is simply to worship God and give alms to the poor: to do this alone in the present situation would be to incur God's wrath.

The pastoral letter then gives several steps that must be taken to transcend the inherited piety and devise a strategy for action. We are told that we must listen to the victims of injustice in our own society. The marginalised must become visible. Christians must speak out to demonstrate their solidarity with them. The pastoral letter recommends a twofold task, one theological and the other social scientific. We must re-read the scriptures to understand them as a message of justice; and we must analyse the causes of oppression and discrimination and participate in actions that try to remove them. This is the episcopal programme to overcome middle class religion. It is not likely that more than a minority of Catholics will take it seriously. It is questionable whether the bishops themselves stand behind their radical pastoral letter.

Notes

1. Quoted in A. Giddens *The Class Structure of the Advanced Societies* (London 1973) p. 177.

2. See J. Bensman and A. Vidich *The New American Society* (Chicago 1971).

3. R. Nisbet *The Sociological Tradition* (New York 1966) p. 216.

4. See M. Harrington *The Other America* (New York 1962).

5. A remarkable pastoral letter, entitled 'This Land is Mine: On Powerlessness in Appalachia', by about twenty Catholic bishops of the region, explores the systematic reasons why the people of Appalachia are trapped in poverty. The pastoral is reprinted in *Redemption Denied: An Appalachian Reader* ed. by F. Guinan (Washington D.C. 1976) p. 200-246.

6. 'A realistic appraisal of the various ideas and behaviour of the American people leads to the conclusion that Americans, by and large, do have their common religion and that this religion is the system familiarly known as the American way of life': W. Herberg *Protestant, Catholic, Jew* (New York 1955) p. 88.

7. Roy Eckart *The Surge of Piety in America* (New York 1958); Martin E. Marty *The New Shape of American Religion* (New York 1959).

8. For an analysis of the entire controversy see *American Civil Religion* ed. by R. E. Richey and D. G. Jones (New York 1977).

9. Neil Bretten *Catholic Activism and the Industrial Worker* (Florida State University 1976) p. 1-16.

10. This task is pursued in a major way by the *Theology in the Americas* project.

Francis Schüssler Fiorenza

Religion and Society: Legitimation, Rationalisation, or Cultural Heritage

FUNDAMENTAL to any discussion of the relation between religion and society is an understanding of the political and social structure of that society as well as an understanding of the historical context and development of the religious beliefs and cultural values of that society. Various perspectives of social analysis can be brought to bear upon the issues of the relation between religion and society. From a Durkheimian perspective, the interrelation between political patterns and religious beliefs can be analysed. The question of the role of religion in relation to the social and political solidarity of a nation or a group can be raised. From a Marxian and Weberian perspective, the questions of the relation between social and economic classes and religious values can be examined. Yet both perspectives remain inadequate and partial if they are not viewed within the context of the social evolution of society and the development and changing patterns of its religious ideas.

In this analysis of the relation between religion and society, I should like to focus on the problem as raised traditionally by Karl Marx and Weber on the relation between social classes and religious beliefs. Since such an analysis is inadequate unless the question is raised whether such a class society or such an analysis based upon class groupings is still valid in contemporary late capitalism or post-industrial society, it will be necessary to discuss theories of the relation between the evolution of society and religious beliefs. It is then finally only in this context that the contemporary relation between religion and society can be understood.

For this reason, it will be helpful to focus *first* on the relation between

24

religion and social class as elaborated by Karl Marx and Max Weber and *second* to discuss the relation between religious heritage and society in view of the work of Ernst Bloch. In this way, the problem of religion and the middle classes in contemporary society can be seen against a broader background of cultural and social analysis.

1. SOCIAL CLASS AND RELIGION

Although the concept of class is central to Karl Marx's thought, he never formally defined what he understood as class.[1] The well-known section at the end of the third volume of *Das Kapital* stops short just when it seemed that Marx would define what he meant by class. Although major elements of his notion of class are borrowed from Saint-Simon, other elements stem from the political economist, Ricardo, and other elements are contained in his historical analyses.[2]

It is important however to note *first* that within Marxian theory the question of class is not merely an issue of the distribution of wealth, but it is also a problem of the distribution of power and influence. *Secondly*, Marx worked out his theory of class in his very attempt to explain the radical transformations of society from traditional to modern social structures. The notion of class is there not just an economic problem, it is also a cultural, social, and political phenomenon that can be adequately understood only with the context of social and political evolution.

In Marx's conception, class society is interrelated with historical evolution. Primitive forms of human society are not class societies. Instead class society is the product of historical change. In primitive societies human beings experience an alienation from nature in so far as they lack mastery over nature. In time, human persons increasingly master nature by means of the division of labour. The alienation of nature is increasingly overcome, but only at the price of the emergence and formation of exploitive class relationships that in turn amount to an even more radical form of alienation. Although *The Communist Manifesto* states that all written history is the history of class struggles, the meaning of this sentence must be correctly interpreted. What constitutes a class is not the same for each type of class society. The development from feudalism to capitalism produces a new system of classes in so far as capital replaces land as the means of production. Class conflict emerges with the incompatibility between techniques of production, the market system of organisation, and other means of social organisation.

Moreover, as Marx's discussion at the end of the third volume of *Das Kapital* indicates, class is not differentiated according to the source of income for then there would be as many classes as there were incomes. Instead of a plurality of classes based upon income, Marx proposes a *dichotomous model*. In each type of society, two basic classes exist: in ancient society, between patrician and plebian, in feudalism, between lord and vassal, and in capitalism between capitalist and wage labourer. The conflict is between those who control the means of production and have political power and those who do not.

The adequacy or inadequacy of this dichotomous model comes into question when this model is concretely applied to history and in regard to religion. Historically and descriptively, the model must embrace the existence of other classes and groupings as Marx himself notes. According to his very own analysis, there exist transitional classes as well as sub-groupings of class. A transitional class may exist in a social structure that has overcome the previous form of that class, e.g., feudal classes within nineteenth-century capitalist states. A transitional class may emerge within a previous societal structure, e.g., the emergence of the bourgeoisie within feudalism. Moreover, sub-groupings exist within the larger class. The petty bourgeoisie as small property owners have different interests from those possessing large means of production. Since the middle class and the petty bourgeoisie fit precisely within these traditional or sub-groups, both the significance and validity of Marx's analysis of the middle class remains controverted.

Nevertheless, this class analysis remains relevant for Marx's understanding of religion and the future transformation of human beings. In the *German Ideology*, Marx writes that 'the ideas of the ruling class are in every epoch the ruling ideas: i.e., the class which is the ruling *material* force of society, is at the same time its ruling *intellectual* force. The class which has the means of material production at its disposal has control at the same time over the means of mental production'.[3] The ruling class seeks to maintain its position in so far as it explains, interprets, and justifies its political and economic domination. It produces a legitimating ideology that reinforces the subordination of the subordinate class.

Marx's understanding of religion can be viewed from the perspective of his analysis of class, even though his critique of religion is much more complex and nuanced than can be perceived from this perspective. Karl Marx does perceive, especially in his early manuscripts, that religion is not only an expression of human alienation, but also a protest against that human alienation, albeit an ineffective protest. Nevertheless, Marx moves beyond Feuerbach's critique precisely because he views it as an abstract critique that views human beings as isolated from their societal existence. The critique of religion must be founded also on a critique of political and social economy. The overcoming of religion and the transformation of humanity are correlated and go hand in hand with a transformation of societal structures.

In this perspective, however, Christianity is related to the bourgeois or middle class. In a market society in which all products become wares and market values, the worker is viewed as an abstract objectified individual. For Marx, Christianity, particular bourgeois middle class Protestantism with its cult of abstract humanity and its belief in person's abstract equality before God represents the correspondent form of religion to a commodity based society. The abstract utilitarianism and individualism of liberal Christianity represents bourgeois ideology. Marx's critique of bourgeois and middle class society is therefore also a critique of liberal Christianity as the ideology of this specific class society.[4] The transformation of the capitalistic class society into a socialistic society demands not only the critique of this society, but also its legitimating ideology. Just as his critique of religion goes beyond the Enlightenment critique and becomes a practical critique.

Weber's analysis of class differs from Marx's description in two ways.[5] First, the differentiation between class and status: Weber distinguishes between social class and status group. This distinction does not simply mean that class is an objective grouping whereas status group is a subjective grouping according to attitudes. More correctly, the distinction relates the classes to production, but divides the status groups according to consumption. The criteria of membership in status groups does not simply flow from the market situation, for status groups represent specific forms of life-style with corresponding ideal and material interests.[6]

Second: the substitution of pluralistic for a dichotomous model. Weber multiplies the number of status groups. Whereas Marx had fundamentally two opposed classes, Weber has a variety of status groups and classes. Various types of middle classes exist between the propertied and the skilled.

Against the background of these two differences, Weber's analysis of the relation between religious ideas and status groups can be seen. He asks which religious ideals were compatible with specific status groups. He sought to demonstrate that specific status groups, for example, peasants, warriors, bourgeois, etc. have interests intrinsic to their occupational status and that the tendencies inherent in their life-styles find their legitimation in specific religious interests, attitudes, and ideals. The dominant values of specific status groups is expressed in the propensities and tendencies within that group toward specific religious ideals and interests.

Weber's correlations are quite well known. *Peasants:* against the nineteenth-century agrarian Romanticism that attributed a high degree of religiosity to the peasantry, Weber argues that those status groups dependent upon agriculture tend toward magic or religious indifference. Their economic interests do not move toward a rationalisation of their religious beliefs for they are bound to nature and dependent on organic

processes. *Warriors:* their life-style obviously does not have any affinity
with kindheartedness or with otherworldly ideals such as sin and humility.
The dignity and courage expected of the warrior stand in contrast to the
virtues of meekness and humility.

As far as the *bourgeois* stratum is concerned, Weber's analysis points
out that the strongly mundane character of the bourgeois life makes it
appear unlikely that much inclination exists for prophetic religion. The
more privileged the commercial class is, the less inclination exists for the
development of an otherworldly religiosity. Individual religious experience tends to be less ecstatic or dreamlike in nature, instead there is more
of a rationalisation of piety. Notions such as duty and recompensation are
present.

In describing bourgeois values, Max Weber clearly distinguishes them
from the values of socialism. He understands under bourgeois two basic
attitudes: the distinctive attitude toward work characteristic of the spirit
of capitalism with its asceticism, dedication, entrepreneural risk-taking
and the individualism which places a premium upon each individual's
own sphere of activity and creativity in the economic and political order.
A rational asceticism and individualism is the distinctive quality of middle
class and bourgeois status groups. A correspondence exists between its
life-style and ideal interests.

2. RELIGION AS CRITICAL CULTURAL HERITAGE

Although Marx and Weber disagree on the issues of the genesis of
capitalism and the relation between the substructure and superstructure,
their descriptions of the middle class are remarkably similar. Both relate
the values of the middle class to the possession of property. Both note a
similarity between puritanism and the bourgeoisie in relation to the
combination of asceticism and active industry. Yet although Marx refers
to the hard work, frugality, and industry of the middle class, he evaluates
its values quite differently from Weber. He speaks of a 'Gospel of
Abstention' as the ideological encouragement of a productivity that
advances the material interests of the bourgeoisie.[7]

This analysis of the middle class and the bourgeois cultural tradition
has come under repeated re-examination. The contemporary view of
present-day society as a late capitalist society challenges the validity of
the above class analysis.[8] Moreover, even neo-Marxism questions
whether the rationalisation of life-style and religious values represents a
rationality that is only a partial rationality that orders means to specific
ends and fails to perceive its own limitations.[9] The most significant critical
corrective is, in my opinion, contained in Ernst Bloch's philosophy of
history. His dialectic of non-contemporaneity not only challenges the

above class analysis, but rejects the wholesale qualification of bourgeois culture as ideology.

The key concepts of this philosophy of history are 'cultural heritage', 'critical non-contemporaneity', and 'critical totality'.[10] They were developed by Bloch in his confrontation with Fascism in order to overcome the deficiencies within Marxist theory. Because Marxism interpreted history and society primarily in terms of economic cause and class analysis, it failed to successfully counter National Socialism in Germany. Fascism is not merely a decadent phenomenon of Capitalism nor the result of economic causes. Instead its success was based upon its ability to use the myths and images of the past and to appeal to the social groupings and structures of the past that protest against the present. Consequently Fascism had an appeal to the middle class and peasantry which socialism did not have. Bloch therefore concludes that the Marxist conception of ideology must be revised. The ideas of the bourgeois class must be seen not merely as the irrational and oppressive ideas of the ruling class, but also as explosive potential for societal transformation.

Within the middle class and its bourgeois ideals, a *cultural heritage* and a *critical non-contemporaneity* exists. A critical tension exists between the bourgeois ideals of the middle class and the middle class reality. A contrast exists between the ideal of the citizens that was intended by the French Revolution and what became of this ideal in the bourgeoisie. An opposition exists between the humanistic ideals of the bourgeoisie and the division of labour within the industrial society developed by the middle class. The ethical ideals of liberalism stand in sharp contrast to their non-realisation.

A prime example of such an ideal that can serve as a critical corrective not only to the middle class society, but also to socialism is the concept of natural law.[11] *De facto* and historically natural law and natural rights have been associated with individualism, with the private ownership of the means of production, and with the dominance of private rights. The Declaration of Human Rights in 1791 revolved around the right of private property which could be called the essential content of the four human rights. Bloch concurs with the socialist critique that natural law is associated with certain illusions, e.g., that rights are innate and not acquired, that they presuppose that individual ownership is prior to common ownership, and that nature is an unchangeable norm. Nevertheless Bloch contends that even though socialism should negate these illusions and the concept of natural law as an abstract and hypostatised ideal, it should not totally reject ideals, at least not, historically and concretely mediated ideals. Therefore it should not reject natural law and natural rights because implied in this law and rights is an affirmation of human dignity. This affirmation is a cultural heritage to be retrieved not only in critique of the present societal conditions, but also with reference to any future society or Utopian conception.

In addition to cultural heritage, Bloch's dialectic of non-contemporaneity has as its other key concept the notion of 'critical totality'. The development of history must not be understood as if earlier stages are simply sublated (*aufgehoben*) into present stages of history. The concept of critical totality expresses a relation to history quite distinct from historicism in which the voice of the past is a voice limited to the specific historical circumstances in which it was spoken. But it also differs from sociological analysis (e.g., Max Weber's ideal types) that views the past merely as examples of typical patterns that are formally identical with present patterns. Critical totality refers to the attempt to understand history so that what has not been achieved in the past is not relegated to the graveyard of historical memory, but serves as a tendency within the present to criticise the present. It is a critical awareness that searches for genuine continuity with the uncompleted past to discover concrete and critical ideals.

This dialectic of history stands in sharp contrast to any one-dimension view of history as progressive. A twofold protest exists within contemporary society. There exists not only a protest against social conditions that arises from a dissatisfaction with the present and is a contemporary protest, but there is also a protest that arises from the past and is a non-contemporary protest. Whereas the contemporary protest feeds upon the dissatisfaction with present in view of future possibilities and is rooted in the objective antagonism between the socialisation demanded by the forces of production and the individualism engendered by the private ownership of the means of production, the non-contemporaneous protest stems from the cultural heritage of the past. Its roots are in the ideals of the past that have not been realised. Its basis is within those classes and groups that have not become totally integrated within modern society. This dialectic underscores the difference between economic liberation and personal liberation as well as between future possibilities and past cultural heritages with their transcendent potentials.

The significance of this view of the dialectic of history can become clearer if it is compared with the recent theories of Jürgen Habermas.[12] He too revises the Marxist notion of class and ideology. Governmental intervention within the economy has changed the power structure so that classes no longer confront one another. Technology as progressive has become an ideology. Nevertheless, he seeks to reconstruct historical materialism by placing on a more abstract level such categories as 'societal work' and 'the history of the human species' and by interpreting them within the context of a theory of social evolution. In this theory the human species undergoes a process of learning not only in technical

knowledge, but also in the development of moral and practical consciousness. Whereas early high cultures have a conventionally structured
system of action and a mythic world view that legitimates domination, the
advanced developed high cultures experience a break with mythic thinking and substitute rationalised world views for mythic world views. In the
contemporary situation that goes beyond the modern period, Habermas
seeks to develop a theory of communicative ethics that goes beyond the
traditional phase of mythic world views and even beyond the bourgeois
phase of a rational world view with its rational natural law. Instead the
possibility for normative decisions regarding human and social liberation
is based upon the possibility of discourse free of domination and upon
formally adequate structures of argumentation.

In this conception religious myths as well as rationalised conceptions of
natural law are sublated and surpassed in the rationality of a communicative ethic. In fact the role of religion is interpreted primarily as
legitimation or rationalisation even where the evolution and development of world views and world images is outlined. But this role is
relegated to a previous historical stage. In what is often called modern
bourgeois society it is relegated primarily to the private sphere.[13] Religion
has become privatised along with metaphysical reason and tradition. In
contemporary society even this privatisation is questioned by references
(e.g., of Habermas) to the 'atheism of the masses'.[14]

Yet the dialectic of history outlined above questions whether formal
rationality or formal structures of discourse can resolve normative questions without reference to substantial cultural values as expressed in
religious traditions. A consensus theory of truth points to the public and
intersubjective nature of truth, but such a consensus is formal and can
represent only a limited rationality despite its apparent universality.
Questions of truth are not only formal issues, but are substantial issues. It
is precisely in the past religious and cultural heritage that substantial
images, values, and visions are present. In this respect the religious
visions and the religious heritage of the past cannot simply be privatised,
sublated, or rationalised within the present. The transcendence of the
religious cultural heritage is a transcendence of substance and content
which contrasts with any non-realisation of its content. Therefore, liberal
views of society that relegate this content to the private realm just as
socialistic views that relegate this content to mere legitimations of class
dominance fails to perceive the vitality as well as need for the religious
cultural heritage.

It was Ernst Bloch's insight that socialism could not meet the challenge
of National Socialism because it failed to take seriously the role of
humanity's cultural heritage. This insight still has its validity. The religious cultural heritage with its visions of humanity and society can be

brought to bear against the utilitarianism and individualism of liberal bourgeois society just as it can criticise a socialism that overlooks and negates this heritage, be it the socialism of orthodox Marxism or the more abstract and formal socialism of the current Frankfurt School. Such a heritage, however, must not simply be repeated, but be analysed for its 'critical totality'.

Notes

1. For discussions of Marx's concept of class see S. Avineri *The Social and Political Thought of Karl Marx* (Cambridge 1968); A. Giddens *The Class Structure of the Advanced Societies* (New York 1975); D. McLellan *The Thought of Karl Marx* (New York 1971) and M. Mauke *Die Klassentheorie von Marx und Engels* (Frankfurt 1970). For critical modifications see R. Dahrendorf *Class and Class Conflict in Industrial Society* (Standford 1959) and S. Ossowski *Class Structure in the Social Consciousness* (London 1963).

2. See esp. *Der achzehnte Brumaire des Louis Bonaparte* and *Die Klassenkämpfe in Frankreich.*

3. *Werke*, Bd. III (Berlin 1962).

4. R. Aschraft 'Marx and Weber on Liberalism as Bourgeois Ideology' in *Comparative Studies in Society and History* 14 (1972) 130-168.

5. Cf. W. Mommsen *Max Weber, Gesellschaft, Politik, und Geschichte* (Frankfurt 1974) and *The Age of Bureaucracy* (London 1977) and C. Seyfarth & W. Spondel *Seminar: Religion und gesellschaftliche Entwicklung* (Frankfurt 1973) esp. the essay by Birnbaum, Löwith, and Giddens.

6. *Wirtschaft und Gesellschaft (Economy and Society)* vol. II.

7. *Capital* I (Chicago 1909) p. 150.

8. Cf. K. Eder *Seminar: Die Entstehung von Klassengesellschaften* (Frankfurt 1973) and in reference to contemporary society for a non-class analysis, D. Bell *The Coming of Post-Industrial Society* (New York 1973).

9. See Habermas's various publications, esp. *Legitimation Crisis* (Boston 1975) (*Legitimationsprobeme im Spatkapitalismus*) and *Zur Rekonstruction des Historischen Materialismus* (Frankfurt 1976).

10. *Erbschaft dieser Zeit* (Frankfurt 1962); first edition was published in 1935. This book contains early essays written in the 1920s in confrontation with National Socialism. The historical dialectic developed in this book underlies much of his later and more explicit analysis of religion in *Das Prinzip Hoffnung* and *Atheismus im Christentum.*

11. Ernst Bloch *Naturrecht und menschliche Würde* (Frankfurt 1961) especially chapter twenty which analyses the Marxist distance to natural rights.

12. *Zur Rekonstruction des Historischen Materialismus* (Frankfurt 1976).

13. Johann Baptist Metz *Glaube in Geschichte und Gesellschaft* (Mainz 1977), esp. chapter three with its theological critique of middle class religiosity.

14. Cf. *Legitimation Crisis* p. 80 'Religion today is no longer even a personal matter; but in the atheism of the masses, the Utopian contents of tradition are also threatened'.

Part II

Theological Perspectives

Wolfgang Stegemann

From Palestine to Rome:
a Social Process in
Early Christianity

CHRISTIANITY BEGAN as a Jewish movement—an internal affair. And it is only recently that we have come to realise once more that in saying this we are not simply making a historical statement about the origins of our faith, which we set apart from Judaism in such an oddly matter-of-fact way. Christianity's roots seem alien to us. But the living conditions of the people who first wandered through Palestine with Jesus are at least equally remote. The people round Jesus included charismatic preachers and healers, who moved about Palestine from place to place. We cannot understand either their preaching or their healing properly—indeed we probably cannot really understand Jesus' own preaching and healing either—unless we relate it to their particular way of life. And we must then go on to relate that way of life to the state of Jewish society at the time.

Jesus and his followers were living in an extremely backward country, which was shaken by political and economic crises. Poverty and hunger, oppression and violence conditioned the life of the lower classes. Hunger and the struggle for the bare necessities of life were the essential problems for most of the Jewish people at this period; and Jesus and his followers faced the same conditions. The earliest traditions about Jesus of Nazareth, which have been passed down to us in the synoptic Gospels, show the wretched conditions of the people clearly enough, and show too that the social crisis in Palestine put its stamp on Jesus' message as well. This is made clear, for example, by his followers' apocalyptic hope for an imminent revolution in existing social conditions, which they saw in subjective terms as hunger for the poor and complacent prosperity for the rich. Jesus and his followers hoped that God would soon reverse all this, compensating the poor for their sufferings and leaving the hands of the rich empty. Jesus says that the poor are already happy, because *they* are the ones who are going to benefit from the lordship of God; whereas a camel will go through the eye of a needle before a rich man enters the Kingdom of God. Poor as they are, the people round Jesus do not feel in any way revengeful towards the rich. They simply believe in God's compensating justice: now it is their turn. The rich have had their share of the good things in life while they were alive. It does not occur to them either to preach 'conversion', *metanoia,* to the rich. They do not feel it to be necessary, because they have no experience of rich people. There were no wealthy men and women in the group surrounding Jesus.

To the Roman-occupying authorities this charismatic movement must have seemed completely provincial. On the other hand the movement itself was probably not focused on Rome or its Jewish governor either. The people to whom Jesus and his friends addressed what they had to say were the Pharisees, for example—i.e., another group which had no power at all at this period. The people whom Jesus and his companions associated with were cripples, the diseased, beggars, tax-collectors and prostitutes—the dregs of society. The subjects of conflict between Jesus and his followers and the people round them also indicate the provincial milieu of the movement. The keeping of the sabbath, or social dealings with the lowest of the low, hardly presented a problem for Palestine's Roman masters, or for their Jewish collaborators. From their point of view, the people surrounding Jesus themselves belonged to the despised groups with whom they identified themselves. Jesus' violent end in Jerusalem in no way contradicts the provincialism of the movement. The fact that he was crucified by the Romans—the fact, that is to say, that they evidently considered him to be politically dangerous—does not mean that he himself was seeking a confrontation with the occupying power. Jesus' crucifixion makes it obvious that this was the execution of someone belonging to the lowest classes. The crucified Jesus was one of many crucified Jews. Moreover his violent end did not necessarily have to attract any more attention to his life and message. In actual fact, therefore, the exact opposite of what Paul claimed to the Roman procurator Festus was true: 'in a corner' was just where Jesus' message was preached and his destiny fulfilled (Acts 26:26). What are undoubtedly the earliest .traditions about Jesus exclude the possibility that his message or the message of his supporters in any way anticipated Christianity's later universal outlook. Even the preaching of the Kingdom of God itself is related to the future of Palestine's poverty-stricken Jews—a future which was viewed as being already present and was soon to be finally implemented.[1]

2.

When we remember this provincial background, it is all the more astonishing that so short a time after his death Jesus' message and Jesus himself could already have become the centre of a religious movement that was positively 'ecumenical', in the sense that it took in the centres of the civilised world of the time. The details of how the Christian movement was able to spread all over the world in this way are obscure. According to the account in Acts, it was in Jerusalem that it first consolidated itself into a kind of independent community inside Judaism. Jews who had returned from the Jewish Dispersion belonged to it, as well as Palestinian Jews. Conflicts with other Jews soon meant that the community of Jesus' followers were driven out of Judaism altogether. Paul's letter to the Galatians and the Acts of the Apostles are basically unanimous in showing that the relationship to the Torah (or to circumcision) became the central theme of conflict in the early church. The beginnings of this problem may already have played a part in Jerusalem (Stephen), but it was in Antioch that it really broke out in all its bitterness. Antioch was the centre of a Jewish Dispersion community, and here a new situation developed as un-circumcised Gentiles as well as circumcised Jews came to belong to the Christian fellowship. It was in Antioch too that the adherents of the movement then came to be called Christians for the first time (Acts 11:26). Paul and Acts think of this conflict as being primarily an internal one. But it is obvious that the special situation of Jewish communities in the Dispersion encouraged both the universal spread of the Christian movement and the gradual process of its separation from Judaism, leading to a critically detached attitude between Christians and Jews that was later to grow into enmity.[2]

This means that when the Christian movement spread from its Palestinian homeland to the *urban* climate outside (penetrating even as far as Rome itself), it did so by way of the Jewish communities who were living in the Dispersion, in the towns and cities of the Roman empire. This made it possible for what was originally a provincial movement to penetrate the region of the Hellenistic cities. The change of religious viewpoint which was bound up with this transition has been exhaustively discussed by exegetical scholars. In the course of this discussion we have become accustomed to talk about a 'Hellenistic' Christianity, as distinct from a Palestinian one. The distinction is really far from precise; but in spite of that it even took on importance for systematic theology. Bultmann, for example, made the 'kerygma' of the 'Hellenistic' church (then represented mainly by Paul and John) the criterion of the Christian proclamation; and this was the chief historical reason why he declared 'the quest for the historical Jesus' to be an illegitimate one.[3] The distinction between the Palestinian origins of Christianity and the movement's development in the urban surroundings of the Hellenistic city churches also plays a considerable part in many theological controversies at the present time, even if this is not always clear to the controversialists. It is all the more important for historical research to draw us a picture of the development of early Christianity—from Palestine to Rome, so to speak—which is unencumbered by any particular dogmatic pre-suppositions. Here the old question about the continuity and dis-continuity of this development will have to take account of the social aspects of the process, as well as its religious side. For if it is true that the religious convictions of the Palestinian followers of Jesus were also directly linked with the special social conditions of this particular region, then the question about continuity or discontinuity becomes a question about the faith, hope and practice of the people who belonged to the Christian movement. That is to say, we have to analyse and compare the *social* content, especially, of Jesus' message and the message of his later proclaimers in the context of the particular social reality in each given case.

3.

The Jesus movement underwent a social development on its way from the province to the cities of the Hellenistic world. A historical account of this process must therefore also take the social history of the time into account. How necessary these enquiries into social history are becomes strikingly obvious when we remember that two very different kinds of early Christian preaching have come down to us and could evidently exist side by side at about the same period—the preaching we find in the apostle Paul's letters on the one hand, and in the 'Logia source' (Q) on the other. This is doubtless connected in part with the particular social realities of the missionary fields in which Paul and the preachers or prophets behind Q were working. Paul was preaching in the towns and cities outside Palestine—the Q preachers in Palestine itself.

The preachers behind Q are the second generation of Jesus' followers. They themselves draw on earlier traditions about Jesus—his calling the poor blessed, for example, which they now apply to Jesus' persecuted followers. Their message is coloured by the special conditions in Palestine between A.D. 30 and A.D. 70, and is consequently very close to the message of the earliest Jesus movement. Fear of starvation or the struggle for existence, the experience of violence and persecution, dread of a violent end, all colour its proclamation to Israel. Their own way of life played a decisive part in this connection, for it was directly connected with their absolute trust in God. Their outward behaviour and their hand-to-mouth way of living was the visible aspect of their message, so to speak, with its exhortations to shake off concern about survival and fear of a violent end through trust in God's loving care. They themselves practised what they preached to Israel: do not worry about your own loves, fear not those who can slay the body. They practised non-violence and love of their enemies, seeing confession of faith in Jesus and corresponding behaviour towards his prophets as the necessary presupposition if Israel is to survive the future judgment. These 'signs' can already be seen, for example, in the bitter divisions within families because of faith in Jesus. The earliest followers of Jesus based their practice on expectation of the lordship of God: God and no one else is lord over the whole of Israel—not mammon, and not the fear of violence, hunger and death; and this divine lordship is already dawning. They did not paint any details of the end of the world, but tried to live in accordance with God's absolute and authoritative claim to the whole of Israel. These Palestinians knew that there were 'Gentile Christians'. But for them this fact is not a particular problem, only showing them anew Israel's guilt with regard to Jesus' message. Their eschatological expectation is universal in that it is founded on a radical idea of God; but it is provincial because it does not consider the fate of people outside Israel at all.

Paul too is a second-generation follower of Jesus. His message, however, has to be understood in the light of the living conditions of the Christian churches in the Hellenistic towns and cities. This area evidently already has its own, independent Christian tradition and it is on this that Paul is evidently building. In Paul the significance of Jesus Christ takes on positively cosmic dimensions. Himself a Jew coming from the important city of Tarsus, Paul develops his Christian theology against the background of a cosmopolitan conception of things. As one who was a Roman citizen himself, he presupposes the political conditions of the Roman empire. Like the people behind Q, Paul is an itinerant preacher. But the different significance of their respective styles of living indicates their different social situations with particular clarity. Paul earned his own living (except on one occasion). He does not hold up his material existence as part of the content of his proclamation; he simply mentions it as proof of his independence. In Q, Jesus' followers claim support from other Israelites because it is their right as prophets. Paul makes the sufferings of his existence primarily a visible aspect of his preaching of the cross, demanding that his congregations follow his example under their *own* conditions. They are not supposed to lead the same life as their itinerant apostle. But for the Q prophets, imitation of their way of life is to be the response to their message. Moreover this is not merely an ethical demand. It must be understood as the offer of an alternative way of living—i.e., an alternative to the power of hunger and violence over men and women. The central task of Paul's life was to build up Christian congregations. It is true that he too probably preached mainly to the lower classes, but their problem is not worry about survival, but the social contempt they met with, even in the churches themselves. The building up of the Christian churches (*oikodomē*), their life together as the body of Christ (*sōma Christou*) with all that meant in actual day to day practice, determines his exhortations. The central content of Paul's message is best summed up by our word solidarity. His eschatological ideas are very close to those of Q, yet they also show the particular background of Paul's experience of reality. Paul thinks of God's rule and of Christ as lord of the world in the universal dimensions of the world-wide Roman empire. The people in Q think of it in the dimensions of Israel. Whereas for Q the false lords who are opposed to God are mammon, fear of starvation and violence, for Paul the powers of the age which are in conflict with Christ and are overcome by him, are sin and death, the destruction of life in the everyday world of the Roman empire.[4]

4.

The Christianity that stands behind the Gospels according to Mark and Luke must be understood in the light of a social world comparable to that of the Pauline congregations. The Gospel of Luke puts us in the fortunate position of being able to observe the reception of the earliest proclamation of Jesus—Q and, to a limited extent, the Pauline kerygma—by an urban Christian congregation at the end of the first century. There are even some indications that Luke had the conditions in the church in Rome in mind. How does the particular situation of this congregation find expression as it comes to terms with the early, and earliest, traditions about Jesus? What special problems in the social life of this congregation emerge from the interpretative reception of the pre-Lucan tradition?

It is noticeable that in Lucan Christianity economic problems were intensified; and in this it differs from the Christianity of the Pauline congregations. There is not only a deep cleft between socially respected Christians and those who were despised; the circumstance that prosperous and wealthy Christians also belong to the congregation is now becoming an important potential source of conflict as well. This is suggested by the unusually critical discussion between the Lucan Jesus and the rich, in many passages in his Gospel. The cleft made by wealth was not always identical with the social one, however. In the story of Zacchaeus, the chief tax-collector, we meet a rich man who is socially despised, but whose behaviour as despised person is a model for the respected rich. On the other hand, though the congregation evidently had needy members, they were not reduced to the bed-rock level (*ptochos*). Luke only knows about the life of the destitute as an outsider, warning the rich that these 'beggars' will enter the kingdom of God in their stead if they do not turn away from their way of life, dominated by their wealth as it is. Luke can no longer imagine that Jesus' disciples were destitute themselves from the beginning. In his writings they only become so because they renounce their possessions, as followers of Jesus. Luke in general puts down renunciation of all but the barest necessities on the part of Jesus' disciples to ethical and religious motives. He does not see it as the result of social realities. In his Gospel the poor are no longer the actors; they are the object of the Christian proclamation and Christian charity. The solidarity of the poor among Jesus' followers becomes in Luke solidarity *with* the poor—by which he means poor non-Christians. So he insists on the Christian duty of alms-giving, meaning by this comprehensive help for the needy. In his opinion this ought to take the place of the 'love between friends', which was usual among equals in Hellenistic society. It is the poor who should be invited to a meal, not the people who can repay an invitation from a wealthy host (friends, relations, rich neighbours).

Luke's handling of the ancient practice of 'love between friends' is an excellent example in general of the link between the religious and the social process as the message of Jesus moved into the region of the Roman cities. The ancient world's 'love between friends' presupposes the social framework of an identical class. Within the same class of prosperous citizens people helped one another and behaved like friends in their social dealings with one another. 'Love between friends' in this sense was bound to be gunpowder in a community of Christians drawn from the most divergent classes, for its exclusive solidarity aggravated the economic and social contrasts in the congregation. Luke has this situation in mind, and demands 'love of our enemies' instead of 'love of our friends'. He picks up Q's message about loving our enemies, but interprets it in the direction of social solidarity between prosperous and respected Christians, and the needy Christians whom they despised. Love of one's enemies becomes, so to speak, the Christian form of the ancient world's 'love between friends'. It is solidarity with the people below, not merely within the same social class any more.

The goal of Luke's message is the abolition of social contrasts through adjustments of material possessions, and the mutual respect of all Christians for one another. He formulates this practical utopia in his account of the church in Jerusalem. It determines the whole tenor and details of his Gospel, which is really a single 'call to repentance' addressed to rich and respected Christians. His eschatology is directly linked with his statements about the social behaviour of Christians. It aims at universal 'peace on earth', which has been within man's reach since the birth of the Saviour of the world (*sōtēr*), Jesus Christ. Without making any direct attack on Roman ruler ideology or on the use of force to preserve the *pax romana,* he manifests the gospel of the true *sōtēr* and of true peace. For Luke the lordship of Christ, as the personal and earthly epiphany of the royal rule of God, has above all broken enslaving power of wealth and social position. And these two powers were the determining factors in the urban life of the Roman empire.[5]

Translated by Margaret Kohl

Notes

1. For my account of the earliest Jesus movement, see the arguments based on literary criticism and social history in L. Schottroff and W. Stegemann *Jesus von Nazareth—Hoffnung der Armen* (Stuttgart 1978) p. 9-53.

2. Cf. A. von Harnack *Die Mission und Ausbreitung des Christentums in den ersten drei Jahrhunderten* (Leipzig 1902) (ET: *The Mission and Expansion of Christianity* (London 1908)). This book is still a valuable source of material on early Christian missions.

3. See here W. Stegemann *Der Denkweg Rudolf Bultmanns. Darstellung der Entwicklung und der Grundlagen seiner Theologie* (Stuttgart 1978) p. 133 ff.

4. For Q see P. Hoffmann's convincing book *Studien zur Theologie der Logienquelle* (Münster 1972). See also Schottroff and Stegemann op. cit., p. 54-88. For the sociological situation in the Pauline congregations, see G. Theissen 'Soziale Schichtung in der korinthischen Gemeinde. Ein Beitrag zur Soziologie des Hellenistischen Christentums' ZNW 65 (1974) p. 232-272.

5. H.-J. Degenhardt *Lukas—Evangelist der Armen* (Stuttgart 1965), is still an important interpretation of Luke's social message in terms of the history of thought. The social-history interpretation I have given here is expounded in more detail in Schottroff and Stegemann op. cit., p. 89-153.

Knud Løgstrup

The Crisis of the Bourgeoisie (*Bürgertum*) and Theology under the Influence of Kierkegaard

1.

THE CRISIS in which the 'bourgeoisie' (*Bürgertum*) finds itself is so very complex that it can be considered, clearly, from many different angles. The line of approach which I have chosen here and to which I intend to confine myself is the tendency to restrict the intellectual horizon to society. A few words, to begin with, on how this tendency has arisen and developed.

The threats and dangers which beset us today on a world-wide scale—with the pollution of the environment, the energy problem and the population explosion—can only be tackled through a far-reaching transformation in the way we organise society and in the international order. More and more people are coming to realise this all the time. Any such transformation ought to be based upon the intrinsic meaning of the universe, the world of nature, and man's being, which we know from our immediate experience. But there is a strong tendency to make the meaning of man's being dependent on the transformation of society, instead of allowing the transformation of society to take its direction from what is already present in man's being. It is thought that if the changes in society are to be sufficiently far-reaching then they must affect the meaning of man's being. But to reverse the order of precedence or priority in this way

43

is fatal, because it means that we are asking of the transformation of society more than it can possibly produce, and if we persist in our demands we shall be left with unyielding dogmas and ideological simplification born of desperation.

In other words, in the political and social spheres we are paying insufficient attention to the basic facts which are already given in the ordering of the universe, the natural world and our own being, and which we cannot change in the slightest degree. The reason for this neglect is that in our western culture we have long ceased to look for the meaning of man's being in those basic facts.

There was a time, not so very long ago, when the question about the meaning of man's being had not yet arisen; it was quite self-evident that the meaning of being was 'given' with what was already there, which no one could alter in the slightest. The question about the meaning of being only arises when it is held not to be permissible to depend upon what exists independently of ourselves.

From the point of view of the history of thought, therefore, the question is not so terribly old—at most a couple of hundred years. Men have tried to answer it with a philosophy of life or view of the world (Weltanschauung). The latter concept stems, as Heidegger observes, only from the middle of the eighteenth century, and he adds that such a phenomenon is unknown and unthinkable in the Greek world, in the Middle Ages, and in the whole of Catholicism. Hans Lipps sees the Weltanschauung as opposed to the scientific view of life, and claims that it has no other point of reference than the individual's own existence. People of the most widely divergent standpoints are at one in this. Bert Brecht observes in his *Ausführungen über Dramaturgie* that it is only when the world finds itself in a state of disintegration that Weltanschauung begins to be spoken of. And Pirandello insists passionately that a philosophy of life or Weltanschauung has no truth-content. His plays demonstrate that what we understand by Weltanschauung has as little to do with reality as the confused ideas of a lunatic. Bertrand Russell does not go quite so far, but he too is unable to accept that a Weltanschauung can mirror reality. This must not be taken to mean that we can dispense with it, since its content reflects what we ourselves want to make of our being.

As Brecht argues, the question about the meaning of being has arisen, paradoxically, precisely at that moment in the history of western culture when we have lost the conviction that we can find the meaning of our living and acting in man's being itself—as it is now understood, independent of our aims and aspirations. But once this conviction has been lost then the question itself has no more meaning. If we start from the proposition that the meaning of man's being is derived from what we do with it, then our opinion determines the meaning, and the meaning cannot outlast the opinion. If it is we who determine the meaning of being then that meaning is arbitrary, and meaning is indistinguishable from meaninglessness. Pirandello is right on that score.

The fact that we cannot dispense with Weltanschauung only adds to our embarrassment. The poets and philosophers we have mentioned are in agreement about its indispensability, while at the same time maintaining that it has nothing whatever to do with truth or falsehood, and that all that we can ask of it is that it should be worthy of us—or at all events not unworthy. But when it is left to our discretion to decide what is worthy and what is unworthy, then we are being asked to drag ourselves up from arbitrariness by our own hair. Although this is impossible we try to do it today, and, as has been said, the method, in our cultural situation, is to make the meaning of being dependent on the transformation of society. At all events this is an important element in the crisis of the 'bourgeoisie', and it strikes so deep that, in this sense, every Marxist belongs to the 'bourgeoisie'.

What then are the basic facts, phenomena and relationships, the non-observance or neglect of which has led to the crisis of the 'bourgeoisie', and which gave man's being its meaning before the question about the meaning of being arose? We may perhaps be led to an answer as we consider, by way of contrast, a view of development which has often been propounded by social scientists. It runs as follows: The development of mankind as a whole has taken place through a great forward-striding process of rationalisation. Progress happens in forward thrusts, as epoch follows epoch, through a continuous growth in knowledge and in man's control over nature and over the social set-up. The first socialising influence in the history of mankind is religion. With myth and worship, with rituals, ceremonies and magic, religion interprets the world and regulates the behaviour of individuals. But precisely because religion is a rationalising factor, it gradually makes itself superfluous. More convincing and effective rationalisations—those of politics, of economics, of technology and of the sciences—outstrip and supersede religion. The process takes quite a while—around two thousand years. But with the period which historians call Modern Times we are at the end of the road: the time of religion is past.

It is clear that my rendering is simplified, by reason of its brevity. But wholly apart from my rendering, the train of thought itself is simplistic. It presents itself as a sort of philosophy of history or development, but completely neglects phenomena which are quite fundamental. Its starting-point is our own knowledge and its objective is the establishment of our supremacy.

What are the phenomena in question? They are many and varied, and I can only enumerate a few of them. First there is speech, which has a capacity for becoming inconspicuous and letting the subject-matter take over, thus giving our understanding, our imagination and our knowledge opportunity and room to unfold. Then there are our sense-perceptions, which interact with our understanding while not allowing themselves in the least to be overwhelmed by it. There is meaning; there is colour. There is a way of understanding which sees behind the thing-and-its-properties and cause-and-effect relationships, and takes us back to the very ordering of the universe itself: the typical leads back to individuals and particular examples, with their own special variations. Then there are the unconditional expressions of man's being, from frankness of speech to compassion.

All these are basic facts, phenomena and relationships in which universe, earth and human existence stubbornly proclaim their singularity. They do not let themselves be absorbed in our activity; they do not let themselves become our end and aim. Hermann Lübbe calls them 'non-negotiable', and goes on to say that they are what religion is about. This does not mean that they have nothing to do with our activity, but rather that they are unconditionally prior to it. Understood in this way they are impervious to our activity.

However they impinge upon our activity in the most varied ways, and can be identified accordingly. There are some—such as time and annihilation, illness, death and suffering—which threaten our activity. In this situation our activity is a form of resistance to the phenomena which threaten it. There are other phenomena which uphold and support our activity—such as trust, frankness of speech, sympathy, hope. It is only because these phenomena do not allow themselves to be tied in with the objectives of our activity that they are able to go on upholding it. We can thus distinguish between two groups of phenomena which are stubbornly independent: the non-negotiable phenomena which threaten our activity, and the non-negotiable phenomena which support our activity. In what follows I shall be concerned exclusively with the latter group.

The question arises as to why we so blatantly ignore them or trivialise them. We do it precisely because we cannot seize them and use them for the organising of society. They cannot be used in this way because, in a sense, they exist for something better—that is, to uphold our being. But we are so much concerned with organising our being that phenomena which cannot be used for that purpose escape our notice. The fact remains that all our organising must be founded on them if it is not to be in vain or lead to destruction.

We must therefore distinguish between those expressions of being which make community life possible and uphold it, and the ideas with which we organise the life of society. We must also consider how they interact and conflict. I shall give two examples of this.

I draw the first from Richard Hansen's article *Spontaneität, Geschichtslichkeit, Glaube*.[1] We would not be in a position to appropriate existing theoretical knowledge, nor would we be able to exchange scientific information, if trust were not an integral part of our being. Nevertheless a distinction must be made. Trust does not come as fully into play in the acceptance of theoretical knowledge as it does in personal relationships, where it acts in a directly spontaneous and sovereign way. In the scientific interchange trust is present more as an idea. This becomes very clear when we think of the 'community of scientists', which plays a very important part in the organising of scientific life, more especially in the exact sciences but also in the realm of theoretical science, as is demonstrated in an article by Peter Skagestad.[2] There is therefore a two-sided relationship between expressions of being and ideas. Trust does not organise. The spontaneous and sovereign expression of being has to do with the organising of our life with or against one another only to the extent to which it is transformed into an idea or gives an impulse to the formation of ideas. At the same time ideas presuppose expressions of being. Without the presupposition of trust as the spontaneous and sovereign expression of being, a 'community of scientists' to organise scientific activity could never have been established.

But the relationship between expressions of being and ideas can be seen in a different and more highly developed form. With my second example we find ourselves face to face with one of our most intractable problems, and I must therefore limit myself to a brief outline. A concept which is characteristic of modern times (in contrast to former times), and which plays an important role today, is the notion of equality Equality, as a concept, can be a fruitful notion so long as it is applied to our involvement in the power structure to which we ourselves are subject. In the ordering of society which we call democratic it is a productive idea. But the notion of equality is a hard and uncompassionate principle if it means that everybody is free to take advantage in whatever way he can of the equality of opportunity which is open to all. If we apply the notion of equality in this way we are acting as though all had equal aptitudes and endowments. In this case equality becomes inequality and gives rise to ruthless competition, the struggle of all against all. How then can we know when the notion of equality is constructive and when it is destructive of life? This is where the expression of being comes in. We can decide on grounds of sympathy and compassion how far the notion of equality is suited to the organising of the life of society and how far it is unsuited.

The same is true in the legal field. All are equal before the law. True. But from ancient times, in the administration of justice, the principle has been recognised that the strict application of the law can give rise to the greatest injustice.

2.

If we pay no attention to the non-negotiable phenomena, then it is clear that their religious application also is lost on us. It might be supposed, therefore, that theology would be against ignoring them. It might be supposed that theology would be innately hostile to that narrowing of the intellectual horizon to society and to the ideas concerned simply with its organisation, which has helped to bring about the crisis of the 'bourgeoisie'. That however would be a great mistake. Theology itself has frequently trivialised those phenomena which do not allow themselves to be taken up into our thought-system and made to establish our supremacy. And just as frequently it has dealt with them in a purely conventional and traditional way and failed to see that the new cultural situation itself might give them a new theological significance. How is this to be explained? The explanation is that it comes from a fear of metaphysics, a fear from which Protestant theology at any rate has been suffering for a hundred years. This fear has a double origin. In part it springs from neo-Kantianism, as is shown by Ole Jensen.[3] In part it originates from the thoughts of Kierkegaard, to which, finally, I now turn.

Kierkegaard's thoughts centre constantly on the point at which the greatest possible contradiction on earth is to be found, because it is at this point that we have to do with the only truth which is worth calling truth. Kierkegaard's point of departure and point of return is, in Climacus' expression, God in time. The remarkable thing is that the religion in terms of which Kierkegaard defines belief in God in time and which provides a frame of reference for such belief, is not that of the God of creation but is rather the religiosity of a Socrates. The obvious course for a man like Kierkegaard, for whom the Christian Gospel is the truth of existence, would have been to turn to the thought of the God of creation and to derive from it a frame of reference for the Christian Gospel. But Kierkegaard does not do that. Why does he not do it?

One of the reasons is certainly the fact that the thought of God in creation, as understood at that time, was associated with traditional metaphysics and the rational theology that went with it. Kierkegaard renounces such metaphysics once for all. His outstanding achievement is that he lays down a completely new foundation. Kierkegaard says: It is useless to try to get anywhere by way of the arguments for the existence of God. For God is already part and parcel of the being of each individual man, before any reasoned argument is advanced, before the mind even starts to reflect on it. Each individual man's relationship to God is given along with his creation. It is superfluous to want to prove the existence of God. The relationship to God is part of the basic structure which underlies the existence of each individual man. Without God, the individual has no being, no existence as man.

This is not the place to pursue the question as to how Kierkegaard develops all this further.[4] The point must rather be made that although in other respects he has made an outstanding contribution—especially when the intellectual climate of his day is taken into account—his analysis of existence is defective in that it gives no place to the notion of creation. Beyond all that is and all that happens, God is only present in man's being as the eternal, infinite, unceasing claim on man. Apart from that there is nothing. There is no room for anything else between the otherness of God and the answerability of man. All else in human life—nature, the universe, whatever exists besides—all that has nothing to do with God. Kierkegaard does not directly deny that God, in his creative and sustaining power, is present in everything that is and that happens—but it is a matter of indifference. For him it has nothing to say. In order to establish the infinite qualitative difference between God and man, and in order to emphasise that his claim is eternal, infinite and unceasing, Kierkegaard is obliged to insist on the otherness of God in such a way that it is achieved only at the cost of the notion of God's omnipresence. This concept has completely disappeared from his field of vision. With Kierkegaard it looks as though God is not at work in creation.

Both the positive aspect of Kierkegaard's argument and its limitations need to be borne in mind. Kierkegaard and the neo-Kantian exponents of dialectical theology were right in rejecting traditional metaphysics and the rationalistic theology that went with it. It sought to extend the scientific method beyond its legitimate limits. That is to say, by describing God as the cause of all that existed, it extended the principle of causality into the beyond.

However, we are limiting the range of our understanding, and depriving it of its proper horizon, if we infer that the theologian is obliged to renounce metaphysics as such. We are also restricting God's claim upon us. Responsible action is then limited to helping one's neighbour to be responsible. Nothing else counts.

In fact there exists a quite different kind of metaphysics from that renounced by Kierkegaard and dialectical theology. It breaks out, as it were, from inside, and is to be perceived in the phenomena of man's being, of the earth and of the universe—phenomena which invite a religious interpretation. It refers us to our immediate experience. And, moreover, phenomena and problems which are open to a religious interpretation open to us in turn the understanding of the Christian Gospel. A faith which has no place for them runs the danger of being a faith without understanding and without consent.

If the content of the Kingdom of God can be expressed in words which we understand, as the preaching of Jesus clearly shows to be the case, then speech in its purely human application cannot be a matter of indifference to God. There would be no place for speech in a world which was pure senselessness and absurdity—senselessness and absurdity which would only be done away in the Kingdom of God. Nor, in gnostic terms, can speech have been created by a Demiurge who mischievously takes pleasure in providing us with a tool with which we can lead one another astray and be at cross purposes with one another. The God of the Kingdom of God must also be the God of speech. Speech must be one of the foundation stones of our being, here on earth.

We find the same thing when we turn from the possibility of speech to more concrete expressions of being. If the Kingdom of God can be depicted in terms of expressions of being through which our togetherness is achieved, then there is no place for such expressions of being in a being of which nothing more can be said than that it is senseless and absurd, and that its senselessness and absurdity will only be done away in the Kingdom of God. The God of the Kingdom of God must also be the God of those expressions of being, and that must leave its impress upon them. In fact it has left its impress upon them: they are marked out by unconditionality and penetrating power.

Translated by G. W. S. Knowles

Notes

1. In *Regensburger Studien zur Theologie* vol. 10 (Frankfurt am Main 1978) p. 42-3.
2. *Making of History* (Oslo 1975) p. 26.
3. O. Jensen *Theologie zwischen Illusion und Restriktion* (Munich 1975).
4. See K. Løgstrup *Auseinandersetzung mit Kierkegaard* (Munich 1968).

Fernando Castillo

Christianity: 'Bourgeois (*Burguesa*) Religion or Religion of the People?

1. IS THERE A REAL DILEMMA?

MANY CHRISTIANS—perhaps most members of the Church—might find it difficult to accept the existence of an alternative between bourgeois (*burguesa*) religion and religion of the people. The fact of a popular religious culture such as exists in Southern Europe and Latin America seems a convincing argument against such a dichotomy. In these societies a Christianity as practised by the wealthy and the social elite (the 'bourgeoisie' or middle classes) exists alongside a popular Christianity belonging to the poorest sectors of the community. Surely such a popular Christianity is proof enough that Christianity transcends alternatives and social divisions, that it is a religion for Everyman?

In this way there would be one sort of Christianity for some and another for others; the one suited to the characteristics of bourgeois or 'modern' society would be more intellectual or 'spiritual', closer to the official structures and practices of the Church; the other would be more emotive, irrational and 'primitive' in its beliefs and practices. Christianity adapts itself to—or, to use the theological term, 'is incarnated in'—particular cultures. (It needs to be said that the proponents of this 'incarnation' usually find no difficulty in fitting Christianity into 'bourgeois' culture; the problem arises when it comes to popular culture.) Everyone, then, finds the Christianity that suits him best. All very straightforward—and in fact very 'bourgeois': everyone consumes (religion) in accordance with his income and place in the social hierarchy.

The 'evidence' for the division of Christianity into 'bourgeois' and popular sectors also rests on a type of social analysis proper to 'bourgeois' society: the division of labour and society itself into classes. This appears to be a natural division, proper to the nature of things. But the problem is not perhaps so simple. The relationship between 'bourgeois' culture and popular culture—in both of which the Church is involved—is in no way politically neutral. It is a relationship between dominator and dominated expressed as the relationship between two cultures. No theory of the cultural incarnation of Christianity can afford to ignore this fact. Once the dominatory nature of the relationship between 'bourgeois' culture and popular culture is recognised, the naturalness of the earlier division disappears. So is the division of Christianity into 'bourgeois' and popular religion a proof that Christianity is above social divisions, a religion for Everyman, or is it rather a sign that Christianity itself displays the contrasts and antagonisms of a world torn apart by contradictions, without calling them into question? The division on the religious level can perhaps be seen as an expression and consequence of the division of labour and society into classes.

This phenomenon can also be seen at work on a world scale, along the lines of the division of labour between rich and poor countries. And what meaning can a religion have if it fails to question these contradictions and merely passively reproduces and reflects them? Metz has already drawn attention to the contradiction within the Church implicit in the hemispherical polarisation between a purely 'bourgeois' religion, for the wealthy and apathetic, and another for the poor, the slaves.[1]

Looking at the matter this way, it becomes clear that popular religion is conditioned by the existence of a 'bourgeois' religion, in the same way that the oppression of the people and their culture is conditioned by the dominance of the 'bourgeoisie' and their culture. Popular Christianity is not exactly a religion *of* the people. The alternative is not posed on this level; popular religion is not the alternative to 'bourgeois' religion, but rather its complement, in the same way that the dominance of the 'bourgeoisie' is complemented by the existence of marginalised and oppressed sectors of the population. In a way, popular religion is the result and expression of the fact that the people are prevented from having their own history, their own culture and Christianity; it is the consequence of the pretended monopoly by the 'bourgeoisie' not only of social and economic hegemony, but of religion and the Church as well.

So one can oppose 'bourgeois' religion and religion of the people. The first would be a religion taken over and neutralised by the 'bourgeoisie' and impregnated with the values of the 'bourgeois' world—class distinctions, human relationships treated as a form of exchange, money as the universal means of communication, etc. The second would be a religious expression of the people's experience of suffering and struggle, a religion that would radically challenge reified values, that could not remain politically neutral in the face of oppression but would take the part of the oppressed, a religion, finally, that would recapture the messianic power of the promise made to the poor.

But the opposition cannot be expressed in these abstract terms, on the level of an 'essence' of Christianity. It has to be expressed on the level of the historical practice of particular individuals. This means that we must look at both the people and the Church, as subjects whose inter-relationship is the key to the nature of Christianity.

2. WHO ARE 'THE PEOPLE'?

(a) *A semantic problem*

'People' is an extremely complex concept, by no means restricted to one meaning. Its understanding presents great difficulties and needs to be approached on various levels. The ambivalent use made of the concept appears in religious language as much as in that of politics and society. 'People' and 'popular' carry a positive or negative charge depending on the ideological bias underlying the usage. (There are also ambiguities in the use of 'people' that are more than purely semantic, originating in the behaviour of the people themselves, in their fragmented and oppressed identity, which makes them easy to manipulate. For example, it was the 'people' who acclaimed Jesus and then shouted 'Crucify him!' (Mt. 21:8-11 and 27:22-5).

In order to clarify the concept of 'people', we need to examine two tendencies relevant also to theological reflection on the people and religion. The first understands 'people' in the sense of '*ethnos*', that is, primarily as an ethnic unity or group. It therefore stresses mainly unity of origin and culture—language, traditions, beliefs, values and institutions. On this basis, this tendency expands sociologically, taking a wide social formation or society, with a common cultural heritage and historical unity, as a 'people'. Politically, this concept is referred to as a 'nation'; in the—not always explicit—logic of this argument, the State becomes the unifying agent and expression of the people-nation.

This view is opposed by another with a different approach; this starts with an understanding of 'people' in the sense of '*plebs*' or '*populus*', the amalgam of groups and social classes occupying a subordinate, non-directive place in society, the oppressed social classes. Again there is a clear political overtone: against the people-nation, challenging it 'from below', from the standpoint of the oppressed, critical and subversive of the order imposed by those in power, those who are not 'people'. This view stresses the opposition between the people and the groups that hold economic and political power. The people exist in contrast and opposition—even if this is not conscious—to the social elite. Here the basic concept is socio-political in nature, but this does not imply that it neglects the cultural dimension: on the contrary, it is just in this line of thought—and only in it—that it is possible for 'popular culture' to acquire real meaning, through its opposition to the culture of the elite or dominant culture. The level of popular culture has in fact a key role to play, since it is the measure of the ability of the oppressed to become practising subjects. But this school of thought insists that culture should always be analysed in relation to the basic socio-political dimension.

The difference between these two schools of thought can be summed up like this: in the first, 'people' is a concept that basically stresses the unity of a social whole; in the second, 'people' underlines the divisions and opposition in this whole—between dominator and dominated. Obviously, it is this second approach that lies behind a theology which poses a Christianity of the people as an alternative to 'bourgeois' religion.[2]

(b) *People, Classes and Culture*

The people constitute the totality of the oppressed classes. This means that their class character will vary with different social formations and the way the class structure develops in them. Latin America is now following the road of industrialised societies, with the emergence of a middle class and a corresponding shift in the basic nature of the people, away from the peasantry of agrarian societies to the urban proletariat characteristic of 'bourgeois' society; the centre of gravity is moving from the country to the city. With this, typically in peripheral capitalism, goes the formation of a sub-proletariat living in shanty towns around the great urban centres. So from a class point of view, the workers, the peasants and the sub-proletariat make up the people. Depending on their position in society and relationship to these central groups, other sectors—parts of the lower-middle classes, for example—could also be included.

This necessarily schematic characterisation of the popular classes also defines the nature of the oppression suffered by the people and its conflict with the national and international ruling classes. The oppression of the people leads inexorably to the problem of the class struggle, that is, to the structural and practical contradictions inherent in the division of society into dominators and dominated. It is only possible to understand the reality of 'the people' in the context of its struggle with the dominant group. The oppression the people suffer is simply the web of structures and practices through which the ruling classes carry on the class struggle 'from above'. The other side of the class struggle is the people's struggle for liberation from this web 'from below'. Theological reflection cannot ignore the fact that the opposition between 'bourgeois' religion and religion of the people takes place in the context of the wider struggle between 'bourgeoisie' and people.

The concept of 'people', however, cannot simply be reduced to 'class', as if it were merely a vague, pre-scientific term for what should strictly be called 'class'.[3] 'People' and 'class' are two concepts on different levels: while 'class' is an essentially analytical concept, 'people' belongs to the practical-strategic level.[4] Here the cultural dimension is of key importance, provided it is not stripped of its class content. Culture is the source, in the form of 'popular culture', from which the people take their immediate identity, even when this identity is fragmented and oppressed by the ruling classes. It is on this level that the people is formed, or opposed and destroyed, as a political and historical subject. This does not mean reducing the practice of the people to purely cultural practice, but taking account of the fact that the actual existence of the people, their conditions of life and work, have their correlation and 'ideal translation' in culture and are processed by the people in their 'popular culture'. The ideal expression can clearly possess illusory and mystifying characteristics which hide and obstruct decisive aspects of its real existence. Even a superficial analysis of popular culture will reveal contradictory traits—of domination, submission and fatalism, but also of resistance, negation of dominating ideas and values, and aspirations to liberty.

The analyses made by Gramsci,[5] especially his concept of hegemony, are particularly useful for understanding these contradictions in popular culture. He shows that class domination cannot be understood exclusively as the capacity to exercise coercion on the dominated classes, but must also be seen as the ability of the ruling classes to create a social consensus, which he calls hegemony. Through their ideological hegemony, the ruling classes influence the practice of the oppressed, neutralising or limiting the forms their struggle can take. Hegemony is the decisive cultural influence exercised by the ideology of the rulers, which penetrates and moulds the overall culture of society, and specifically of popular culture too. So if the hegemony of the ruling elite is highly developed, the ability of the oppressed classes to articulate themselves as 'people' is suppressed or neutralised. This would explain why, when the working classes in wealthy societies are 'bought' by the consumer society and by the ideology of consumption, they cease to be 'people'. Conversely, the existence of 'a people' is a sign that there is still a problem of hegemony which the rulers have not resolved, a hegemony somehow called into question. The more it is questioned, the greater the strength of the presence of the people as historical subject.

Gramsci's approach shows the contradictions in popular culture as the expression of an ideological hegemony incompletely imposed by the ruling classes on the people. It avoids any sort of romanticism or populism in its view of popular culture. Romantic idealisations leave the concept of hegemony out of account; the immediacy of popular culture then appears to represent the authentic being, the real essence of the people, taking no account of the fact that what is really being discovered is largely the rulers infiltrating the people, a cultural invader forcing its ideology on strategic areas of popular culture, disorganising and fragmenting it, preventing the people from building a coherent identity for themselves. Popular culture is the field in which the symbols produced by the people are voided of content and expropriated by the hegemonic influence of the ruling classes. This does not mean it is a mere artefact of the rulers imposed on the people. Popular culture is still an articulation of the people's resistance, hopes and struggle for liberation. Precisely because it is not an arbitrary elaboration, but at the same time the expression of the existence and aspirations of the people as well as the voiding and transformation of these symbols to their detriment, popular culture is the ground on which the ruling bloc can obtain the consent of the people; it is the territory open to infiltration and capture 'from inside', where the people can be manipulated from the basis of their own consciousness. Precisely because of this, it is also the ground from which the people can articulate their resistance and struggle for freedom.

3. THE CHURCH AND THE PEOPLE

The Church, acting as subject and institution, is the standard-bearer of Christianity in history. The type of Christianity existing in a given society is the result of a particular mode in which the Church has proclaimed the Christian message and of the specific manner in which this proclamation has related theory to practice. This makes the relationship between the Church and the people decisive in deciding whether Christianity will be a 'bourgeois' religion or a religion of the people. Analysis of this relationship should start from a concept of the Church purged of the lyrical idealism, so common in ecclesiology, which seeks to define the nature of the Church solely on the basis of concepts and grants itself a dispensation from examining its social behaviour and political significance as an institution. If theology is not to deceive itself on the Church as 'people' (of God) and as a supposedly Christian people, it should take account of the gap that has grown up between the Church and the people. This gap is the result of the history of both the Church and the people in recent centuries.

Without claiming to reconstruct this history, one can simply say that the Church has allied itself with the powerful, woven itself into the fabric of domination, absorbed the world-view, values and ideologies of the ruling classes. Despite this, in Southern Europe and particularly in Latin America, the Church has kept a close relationship with the people. It is particularly clear in Latin America that the relationship between the

Church and the people has been marked by a dialectic in which, on one side, the Church which came with the colonisers—and even because of its symbiosis with them—has been a major factor in the promotion and development of popular culture, thereby contributing to the formation of the people, not only as alienated and oppressed, but also as seekers of and fighters for liberation; on the other side, the history of the Church as an institution tied to the ruling classes has moved away from the people and their struggle for liberation. The result is a situation in which the Church is a Church of the elite, while Catholicism is a religion of the people.

The two phenomena are not contradictory. The Church of the elite, as a cultural apparatus, has played an important part in developing and maintaining the unity and ideological coherence of society, from above. From a socio-political point of view, it has functioned as a channel of communication from the elite to the people, and therefore as a means for the expansion of the hegemony of the elite. But this does not happen without grave consequences for the Church and for Christianity. The people, despite their religious feeling, feel uncomfortable and even out of place in the Church. The Church is confronted with a popular Christianity permanently demonstrating its suspicion of the official rules and practices of the Church; the people have their children baptised and wish their dead to have a Christian burial, but they do not go to mass and are reluctant to listen to any message from the Church; they see the Church as the administrative arm of 'religion', to which respect must be paid, but they do not feel they belong to it and they understand little of official religious teaching. 'Christians', for their part, i.e., those lay people who take part in the activities of the Church and identify themselves most closely with it, are not drawn from the ranks of the people, but from those of the elite or of intellectuals close to the ruling elite.

In the last few decades, however, this situation has begun to change rapidly and profoundly. Ever more numerous sectors of the Church, of growing importance, both lay people and priests, are seeking to draw closer to the people to become part of their existence, sharing in the poverty of their lives and the hardship of their labours, their afflictions and sufferings, and becoming steadily more committed to their struggle for liberation. (Similar processes can be seen at work elsewhere, such as in Spain, where sectors of the Church made a decided commitment to the final phases of the struggle against Francoism.) This shift of sectors of Christians toward the people has taken place in a context of the birth of a new consciousness in the people, marked by a growing understanding of their structural situation of oppression and by increasingly clearer and more precise aspirations to overcome it; it is a context in which the people are rising up, with a strength hitherto unknown, as a subject seeking to be the protagonist of a new history of freedom in Latin America. As

Gutiérrez[6] has observed, Christians who take on this commitment undergo the experience of entering a new world, that of the poor, which has up till now not been the world of the Church. Through practising this solidarity with the people, Christians have learnt to look at the world from the standpoint of the people, and have become conscious of the whole network of social relationships that bind them into a situation of exploitation. This has had its effect on the faith of these Christians; political commitment to the liberation of the people is also an experience in faith. They discover the deep convergence between the radical nature of Christian choice of the poor and the radical nature of the political praxis of liberation. Mysticism and politics come to be seen as two faces of the specific experience of loving one's neighbour.

This shift of sectors of the Church has also produced a relative shift in the Church as a whole; more precisely, it is producing a Church on the side of the people, a Church that defines itself on the basis of its commitment to the people, no longer sharing the history of victories of the powerful, but the history of suffering and liberation of the people. One sign of this, a sad one but full of hope for the future, is the persecution the Church is suffering in the cause of justice. There is now a large number of bishops, priests and lay people who have been tortured, assassinated or imprisoned by regimes that call themselves 'Christian'. These martyrs are the seeds of a new Church, one that shares the fate of the people.

4. POPULAR RELIGION AND THE CHRISTIANITY OF THE PEOPLE

What happens to popular religion in this process? What place can it occupy in the growth of a new Church and a Christianity of the people? One needs to beware of two simplistic attitudes toward popular religion. The first is abstract criticism which disqualifies popular religion as mere superstitious degradation or as mere ideology of domination obstructing the development of the consciousness of the people. In this view, popular religion has no part to play in the formation of the Christianity of the people. The second is the naïve and uncritical euphoria which sees the people of Latin America as being profoundly Christian, where in lies the solution of all problems: as long as the people go on being religious they will have no worries and neither will the Church; the task of the Church is to maintain and 'purify' the religion of the people. What both views have in common is the reduction of religion to religious feeling, isolating it from social practice.

The truth, however, is probably that all the complexities present in popular culture are heightened in the realm of popular religion. Its symbolism expresses the history of the oppression and hopes of the people with a special intensity—and this symbolism is at once voided and taken over by the dominant culture. Popular religion undoubtedly contains an element of religious alienation, of a religion that displaces hope and obfuscates the historical embodiment of faith and charity. But it also contains an immense potential for liberation: the historical strength of a faith that knows—silently—that Jesus was poor and that God is with them; a faith that has helped the people to resist—not just to put up with their history of oppression.

The growth of a Christianity of the people must necessarily start from the—doubtless ambiguous—basis of popular religion, just as its historical and political identity starts from the basis of popular culture. Removing oneself from it means removing oneself from the real existence of the people; remaining in it means nourishing a religious populism that reproduces the ambiguity. . . . Under what conditions, then, can popular religion be transformed into Christianity of the people? The formula commonly found in Latin America, 'evangelising popular religion', even though it contains an important truth, is inadequate, since everything depends on the way in which 'evangelisation' is understood. Does it mean 'purifying' popular religion so as to bring it into line with official religion, the religion of the elites? Is it simply a matter of bringing the people to the religion of the Church? Evangelisation should be seen as a process in which proclamation and practice are combined, and in which practice plays the decisive role. Evangelisation supposes a specific evangeliser with a particular practice and position in society. This brings us back to the main point: there can be no Christianity of the people without a Church of the people; only such a Church will be in a position to evangelise popular religion, transforming it and making it mature into a Christianity of the people.

This Church of the people is arising in Latin America. The choice made by sectors of the Church for the oppressed is not yet the Church of the people, but it is a living seed that has begun to bear fruit in the emergence of innumerable Christian communities that really are 'base' communities of the people; communities in which peasant, worker and settler are united in their commitment in faith and struggle for liberation, in which they live and reflect this commitment. This is where those sectors of the Church that have opted for the people find their integration with the people, where they too become people. This is the Church whose praxis of solidarity with the people and proclamation of liberation to them is giving shape to a Christianity of the people. Here is the chance for a people to build its identity and its history of liberty on faith in Jesus Christ, man of the people and Lord of history, and for a Church that is 'people' to arise.

Translated by Paul Burns

Notes

1. See J. B. Metz *Glaube in Geschichte und Gesellschaft* (Mainz 1977) p. 128.

2. Here I frankly disagree with J. C. Scannone ('¿Vigencia de la sabiduría cristiana en elethos cultural de nuestro pueblo: una alternativa teológica?' *Stromata* 32 (1976) No. 3/4 pp. 253-87), who, starting from a definition of 'people' as a 'historico-cultural' category, takes the 'people-nation' line. He sees 'people' as a political category since the cultural community 'is capable of forming itself into a State' (p. 257).

3. The nature of a 'people' of the middle classes (a problematical category in itself) cannot be established *a priori*; it depends on structural and situational factors. There are groups usually included in the 'middle classes' which are structurally integrated into the ruling class and have nothing to do with the people (upper civil servants, for example). There are other groups whose situation places them closer to the oppressed classes but who can still develop an extremely anti-popular ideology and attach themselves to the ruling clique.

4. See N. Poulantzas *Les classes sociales dans le capitalisme aujourd'hui* (Paris 1974).

5. On Gramsci's concept of hegemony, see M. A. Macciochi *Poux Gramsci* (Paris 1974) and L. Gruppi *Il concetto di egemonia in Gramsci* (Rome 1972).

6. See G. Gutiérrez *Evangelio y praxis de liberación: Fe cristiana y cambio social en América Latina* (Salamanca 1973) p. 234.

Johann Baptist Metz

Messianic or 'Bourgeois' Religion? On the Crisis of the Church in West Germany

TO ISSUE critical diagnoses of such a well organised and internationally highly regarded religious community as Catholic Christianity in West Germany is in itself a delicate venture. The problem becomes more difficult when what is attempted is to show that the critical area is none other than the one in which Christians in these parts seem most at home, in the comparatively large degree of harmony between the practice of religion and the experience of life in society.

The critical hypothesis which we shall try to substantiate in what follows begins with this question: Is Christianity in West Germany in the end a bourgeois (*bürgerliche*) religion—with great social value but without a messianic future?[1]

1. BOURGEOIS FUTURE—MESSIANIC FUTURE

When the Church in West Germany repeats the messianic sayings about the Kingdom of God and the future it represents, it is speaking in the main to people who already have a future. We could say that they bring their own futures to church with them, the strong and unshakeably optimistic to have it religiously endorsed and rounded off, the anxious to have it protected and strengthened by religion. In this way the messianic future frequently becomes a ritual rounding off and transfiguration of a 'bourgeois' future already worked out and—as death approaches—an extension of this 'bourgeois' future and the ego which thrives in it into the transcendence of eternity. *In the Christianity of our time the messianic*

religion of the bible has largely become 'bourgeois' religion. This observation is not intended as a denunciation of the 'bourgeois'; his social role
is not as such our subject. Nor is it primarily a criticism of the fact that the
Church in Central Europe consists mainly of the so-called 'petty
bourgeoisie' and 'bourgeoisie', who set the tone of Church life in our own
country too. It is more the expression of a worry about Christianity,
which, it seems to me, loses its identity if it does not realise and emphasise
its difference from 'bourgeois' religion.

In this 'bourgeois' religion the messianic future is in the gravest danger.
Not in danger of being alienated and becoming a tranquilliser or a con-
solation, an opium for the have-nots, for those with no future, but of
turning into an endorsement and encouragement for the haves, the
propertied, for those in this world who already have plenty of prospects
and future.

The messianic future of Christian faith does not just endorse and
reinforce our preconceived 'bourgeois' future. It does not prolong it, add
anything to it, complete or transfigure it. It *disrupts* it. 'The first shall be
last and the last shall be first.' The meaning of love cuts across the
meaning of having: 'Those who possess their lives will lose them, and
those who despise them will win them.' This form of disruption, which
drops like a bomb on our complacent present, has a more familiar biblical
name; 'repentance', turning of hearts, *metanoia*. The direction of this
turning is also marked out in advance for Christians. It is called *discipleship*. We must remember this if the future for which faith fits us is not
to be interpreted in advance in terms of 'bourgeois' religion—or, in other
words, if we do not want simply to replace the messianic future with our
own future, the one in which we are well in control.

2. THE CHANGE OF HEART IS NOT TAKING PLACE

To change states of affairs is said not to be the concern of the Gospel
and not the business of the Church, which seek to change hearts. This is
true and false at once. The moving of hearts is in fact the first step to the
messianic future. It is the most radical and most demanding form of
reversal and revolution, and it is so because changing states of affairs
never changes all that really needs to be changed. But this also means that
this change of heart is certainly not an invisible or, as people like to say,
'purely inward' process. If we are to trust the Gospel testimonies, it goes
through people like a shock, reaches deep down into the direction of their
lives, into their established system of needs, and so finally into the states
of affairs which that helps to shape. It damages and disrupts one's own
interests and aims at a revision of familiar practice.

I want to express the fear (again not as a denunciation, but uncertainly and with sadness) that *this change of heart is not taking place*—at least not in the form in which it is publicly proclaimed. The crisis (or the disease) of life in the Church is not just that this change of heart is not taking place or is taking place too little, but that the absence of this change of heart is also being obscured by the appearance of a mere belief in faith. Are we Christians in this country really changing our hearts, or do we just believe in a change of heart and under the cloak of belief in a change of heart remain the same? Are we disciples or do we just believe in discipleship and under the cloak of belief in discipleship continue in our old ways, the same old ways? Do we love, or do we believe in love and under the cloak of belief in love remain the same egoists and conformists? Do we share the sufferings of others or do we just believe in sharing them and remain, under the cloak of a belief in 'sympathy', as apathetic as ever?

It is no theological answer to these questions to stress that, after all, repentance is grace. Theology should take particular care that this appeal to grace does not slip into that leniency we show ourselves, that it does not simply become confused with that indulgence we show to our own bourgeois hearts. The same applies to the objection that such a criticism of contemporary Christianity ignores the sin in which Christians continue to be trapped. Clearly theological talk about sin and the forgiveness of sins must not be arbitrarily separated from the messianic call for a change of heart. And then when people insist that this change of heart is in the end a purely 'inward process', that is certainly not an article of faith but entirely an ideology of our 'bourgeois' religion with which we conceal from ourselves yet again our failure and refusal to change.

A '"bourgeois" theology' assists this concealment. For example, in its theological discussion of the last things the messianic future was long ago freed from all apocalyptic tensions: there really are no dangers, no contradictions, no downfalls left. Everything is dominated by the idea of reconciliation. But by taking this line this bourgeois eschatology unconsciously gives our present a certificate of moral and political innocence, reinforces this 'bourgeois' present in itself instead of pushing it beyond itself: everything will be all right in the end anyway, and all differences reconciled.

In this process hope in 'bourgeois' religion steadily loses its messianic weakness, the fact that it still expects something. But the price hope pays for being detached from expectations which could ever be disappointed is high! Hope becomes a hope without expectations, and hope without expectation is essentially hope without joy. I think this is the source of the joylessness of so much joy in 'bourgeois' Christianity.

Love in 'bourgeois' religion, too, it seems to me, loses more and more of its messianic character. Messianic love is partisan. There was certainly a privileged group around Jesus—those who were otherwise underprivileged. The universality of this love does not consist in a refusal to take sides, but in the way it takes sides, without hate or personal hostility—even to the folly of the cross. Is there not a concept of universal Christian love in 'bourgeois' religion which is just sloppy, and one which hardly needs any longer to prove itself as love of enemies because the feeble and un-partisan way it bridges all the agonising contradictions means that it has no opponents left at all?

Under the cloak of 'bourgeois' religion there is a wide split within the Church between the messianic virtues of Christianity which are publicly proclaimed and ecclesiastically prescribed and believed in (repentance and discipleship, love and acceptance of suffering) and the actual value-structures and aims of 'bourgeois' practice (autonomy, property, stability, success). Among the priorities of the Gospel the priorities of 'bourgeois' life are practised. Under the appearance of the belief in repentance and the belief in discipleship, the 'bourgeois' subject is set up—with an absence of contradiction which even it finds uncomfortable—with its interests and its own future.

If I am right, Kierkegaard's critique of 'Christendom' can be taken as an early form of criticism of 'bourgeois' religion in Christianity. Kierkegaard claimed that 'Christendom'—without attracting attention and even without noticing—had more or less identified Christian existence with the 'natural' existence of the 'bourgeois': the Christian practice of discipleship was covertly transformed into 'bourgeois' practice. In the shape of 'Christendom', Christianity had once again successfully and quasi-triumphalistically come to terms with the power of the prevailing society, in this case with that of 'bourgeois' society. But at what price? No less, says Kierkegaard, than the abolition of Christianity itself, the Christianity of discipleship, as he keeps on insisting. I regard this is an early critique of Christianity as a 'bourgeois' religion which is in the full sense prophetic and not at all obsolete today, but—for Catholics and Protestants—more urgent than ever.

3. RIGORISM INSTEAD OF RADICALISM

The bishops feel the dangers which the 'bourgeois' religion as practised contains for the life of the Church. They are aware of the danger that the Church will not so much move the hearts of the 'bourgeois' as be changed by the 'bourgeois' into an institution of 'their' religion, a service-Church to supply their security requirements. *Nevertheless our Church's pastoral approach to 'bourgeois' religion tends, in my view, to be based on resignation*, a strategy of latent distrust, fed by the suspicion that the 'bourgeois' is not in the end to be trusted, that ultimately he would overwhelm Christianity with his priorities and preferences if there were relaxation even at one point. So the bishops react with legal rigorism in those cases in which actual or supposed truisms of 'bourgeois' society come into most evident conflict with the preaching of the Church, as in the question of divorce or the readmission of divorced people to the sacraments, in questions of family and sexual morality, and lastly in the matter of compulsory celibacy, to mention only these examples. This is not an attack on the Christian ideal of monogamy or a plea for sexual libertinism or an attack on the eschatological-apocalyptic virtue of celibacy. The question is simply whether such legal rigorism is the way to overcome the contradictions of 'bourgeois' religion in Christianity and make the Christian alternatives to a life which has become 'bourgeois' really visible. Or, to put it an other way, whether this is the way to heal the split between the messianic virtues of the Gospel which we preach and those which the 'bourgeoisie' practise, i.e., whether repentance for discipleship is possible.

The main fault of this rigorism with which the official Church reacts to the crisis and disease of Church life implied by 'bourgeois' religion is that it seems to be no real help to the base, to the average parish. It is the parishes which have to bear the full weight of this contradiction. It is here that it is becoming clear that the rigorism of the Church offers no salvation in the battle against the distortions of 'bourgeois' religion if the radicalism of repentance is not faced and risked in common.

In the local community the contradiction between the messianic virtues of Christianity which are preached and the 'bourgeois' ones which are actually lived is particularly painful. The 'bourgeois' virtues of stability, the competitive struggle and performance obscure and crush the messianic virtues of repentance, selfless and unconditional love for the 'least of the brethren' and compassion, which receive only notional assent— virtues which cannot be practised in exchange relations, for which you get, literally, nothing, like the love which does not insist on recompense, loyalty, gratitude, friendship and mourning. They have a diminishing existence and are at most—under the division of labour—devoted to the family, which in turn is coming more and more under the pressure of social exchange processes.

In the family, the sector to which the Christian virtues in their privatised form are allocated, the contradictions are becoming blatant. Here love has, as it were, to be reduced to a love which sacrifices universal justice. *But where Christian love is lived only in the family, it soon becomes impossible to live even there.* Like celibacy, the Christian family is tending too much to develop into an isolated mode of life, exactly the same tendency which is present in 'bourgeois' society.

Of the alternative, discipleship lived in practice, there is no sign. The more difficult it becomes to conceal this contradiction with the Gospel, the more emphatic the ecclesiastical appeals seem to become which present the family and celibacy as islands of Christian virtue—and, it seems to me, the greater the danger to them from legal overloading.

The 'family' model of the parish is threatened by the same fate which already seems to have overtaken the family. It is losing its young people or is no longer able to integrate them with their criticisms, their alternative attitudes and their experiments in political emancipation. And yet there are young people waiting for the call to discipleship, there is a longing for radical Christian existence, for alternatives to 'bourgeois' religion. If these young people are becoming increasingly hard to reach, if they are gradually going away to other struggles, the fault is not theirs alone.

If the term '"bourgeois" religion' is justified, this will become particularly clear in the role which *money* plays in it. Money is, after all, a tangible symbol of 'bourgeois' society, and the principle of exchange which governs it down to its foundations. An examination of the function of money in a 'bourgeois' religion involves more than looking at the semi-ideological status of Church tax. The main issue is the compensatory function which money in general has acquired. One aspect is its use by the Church authorities, where fines are instituted as a disciplinary measure and money becomes almost an aid to the maintenance of ecclesiastical orthodoxy. More important, however, is the salvational function of money for Christians in general. Money, often acquired totally without compassion, becomes a substitute for compassion with the suffering of others; it serves to express solidarity and sympathy, as compensation for the neglect of a wider justice which is imposed by a society determined at a fundamental level by exchange. Money thus becomes the great link between the Christian virtues, which in 'bourgeois' religion are kept strictly to the private sphere, and social suffering; it becomes *a quasi-sacrament of solidarity and sympathy*. Even then—in its quasi-sacramental role—it still expressed something of what, in my view, it cannot provide, the direction and spread of our love and compassion by those messianic standards for which there are really no limits to liability. The problem of the big Church charities is not that they exist, but that, in the minds of the Christians of our country, they take the necessary help out of the wider messianic context (which includes factors like solidarity, political education and a desire for practical change) and reduce it to a process of mere monetary contributions.

4. RADICALISM INSTEAD OF RIGORISM

I start from the presumption that the reason for the Church's loss of appeal is not that it demands too much but that in fact it offers too little challenge or does not present its demands clearly enough as priorities of the Gospel itself. *If the Church were more radical in the Gospel sense, it would probably not need to be so 'rigorous' in the legal sense.* Rigorism springs from fear, radicalism from freedom, from the freedom of Christ's call. For the Church's preaching and pastoral work, acting by the priorities of the Gospel should include using the all-embracing strategy of love to attack the ideal of exchange as it seeps down to the moral foundations of social life. It means overcoming the reification of inter-personal relations, their increasing interchangeability and superficiality. If it does this the Church is radical without necessarily having to be rigorous in the legal sense. If it did this, for example, it could admit to the sacraments even those who had failed in their marriages and asked for forgiveness, without having to fear that it was opening the floodgates. Nor would the Church then need compulsory celibacy to dress up a Christianity which had lost its radicalism. There would be no danger that the apocalyptic virtue of celibacy would die out; it would constantly re-emerge out of the radicalism of discipleship.

Then, too, authority in our Church would lose the bureaucratic face which everyone complains about: it would be able to take on more clearly the features of an authority for religious guidance, display its administrative and legal competence less and its religious competence more.

5. POLITICS, MORALITY, RELIGION: THE WORLD CONTEXT

How can we bring about a shift in priorities? How can we achieve a renewal which will affect even the psychological foundations of 'bourgeois' life? I myself see only one way here: we need *a change of direction throughout the Church, throughout society and in the whole of world politics.* This is not a detour or an escape into undemanding abstraction. What is much more of an abstraction today is the approach which 'abstracts' from the world-wide connections in which our individual and social life is involved.

Our world, for the first time aware of itself as a whole, is at the same time riven with deep, agonising *oppositions*, which threaten more and more to become an apocalyptic gulf between poor and rich, rulers and ruled. Purely political or economic strategies for ending these oppositions are either not in sight or are proving inadequate, only with difficulty covering up the apparent irreconcilability of the interests. This makes many people bewildered and apathetic, and drives others into hatred and fanaticism (a much more likely result of our ubiquitous apathy than a conversion to committed love). Others again take up rigid defensive attitudes and end by adopting a strategy of self-preservation and internal security.

Everyone can see the signs of this looming social apocalypse: the atomic threat, the insanity of the arms race, the destruction of the environment, terror, the global struggle for exploitation (the North-South conflict) with its danger of a social war on a world scale. And yet the catastrophe remains mostly ideas 'in the head', not in our hearts. It produces depression, but not grief, apathy but not opposition. People seem to be becoming more and more voyeurs of their own downfall. Counter-measures are scarcely to be seen, probably because the familiar strategies and prophecies are failing.

It is certainly not my intention here to mystify 'the catastrophe' or to ridicule any nuance, any sign of an initiative, by some slick juggling with the idea of the totality of the disaster. Quite the opposite. My only aim is to see that we appreciate the scale and nature of the action which has become necessary. Must we not start from the assumption that the oppositions which are producing hatred and despair or apathy can only be overcome without a catastrophe when there is a change in personal priorities in the rich countries of this earth (and not just among the grabbers within the oppressed nations who have grown rich through their ruthlessness), in other words, when there is a real change of heart here? Is this not the only way in which the poor and exploited can escape from their damaged lives, stunted as they are from the very beginning? *Is not moral action becoming a factor in world politics?* Or, to put it the other way, are not economics and politics becoming part of morality in a new way?

Christians are convinced that such a moral reorientation cannot be kept up unless it is supported by religion. They start from the assumption that where religion not only disappears among the so-called enlightened élites, but even among the people the report of the existence of God is no longer abroad, man's very 'soul' dies, and in the end the apotheosis of banality or hatred dawns. The individual becomes a machine, a new sort of beast, or just an offence, to be dealt with by totalitarian means. It is precisely for these reasons, in view of the situation I have described, that Christianity with its moral reserves and its capacity for repentance is called to stand the test of history. *It is my view that nothing is more urgently needed today than a moral and political imagination springing from a messianic Christianity and able to be more than just a copy of accepted political and economic strategies.*

6. THE CHURCH'S WORK OF RECONCILIATION

The Church's international character provides us with a dramatic illustration which focuses on this situation and the challenge it contains, or the call for a change of heart which rises out of it. This is the relation of the rich churches to the poor churches, let us say, *of the German-speaking churches to those of the Latin American subcontinent*.

I am not placing the question of repentance in the context of the international Church in order to have an imaginary parade-ground for aesthetic radicalism. This is no abstract speculation about the future, but a practical question: Have others, namely our fellow participants at the eucharistic table in the one Church, even a present? We can forget about the future completely for the moment!

This concern with the Church internationally should also have another effect. I am convinced that there will only be a reconciliation between the traditionalist wings and the more liberal wings of our European Church if the Church's work of reconciliation makes its main task reconciliation between the poor and rich churches as a whole, and so makes a contribution to the reconciliation of our painfully torn world. In other words, the goal of sanctity must be linked with that of militant love.

These poor churches have already given us this new model of Christian life. They have given it to us in the witness of those countless Latin-American Christians who have lived the messianic virtues of discipleship to the extent of sacrificing their lives. They are the productive model of sanctity for our time, sanctity, not as a strictly private ideal, which one seeks for oneself and which can therefore easily lead into conformism towards the existing situation, but sanctity which proves itself in an alliance of mysticism and militant love, which takes the suffering of others on itself. Our time certainly has a martyrology of its own. It contains the names of the lay people, priests and bishops who have risked all and given all in the struggle for a Church with the people. With them, these allies united by messianic confidence, repentance becomes possible; the spell of 'bourgeois' religion is broken. Such a perspective shows how little the current priorities in the life of the West German Church are simply the natural priorities of a church; it shows that there can be quite different pastoral priorities from those which are central in this country.

There is taking place in the Churches of Latin America a change of direction on a massive scale, which in my view has a providential significance for the whole Church and in which, in one way or another, we are all involved. In the last ten years (since Medellín) an upheaval has been going on there which could be described as the change from a Church which ministers to the people to a Church of the people. The suffering and oppressed people are finally becoming the masters of their history—not in opposition to the Church or by ignoring the Church, but through the Church and in the power of its messianic hope. It could therefore come about that there one day not just the oppressed people, but also the victorious people, could become part of the Church! It is of course true that Christian hope exists even in a life under oppression. The messianic hope of Christians is, after all, much more a hope of the slaves and the damaged of this earth than a hope of the victors. But the 'successful' and prosperous Christians are the last people this entitles to argue for a strictly interiorised version of Christian hope which they then impose on the poor churches.

And it is just the Central European, 'bourgeois' religion of interiority which influential cardinals, bishops and certain working-parties in my country seem to want to be the new standard for the Medellín Church in Latin America. This vision fills me with fear and makes me ask whether the cost to Latin America of all the alms is not indeed out of this world.

Sharing the fate of these churches challenges us here to change. Only if we change will Christians here be able to show help and solidarity. The direct struggle of the poor and oppressed people there must be matched here by struggle and resistance against ourselves, against the insidious ideals of always having more, of always having to increase affluence. It must be matched by a struggle against the over-determination of the whole of life by exchange and competition, which only permits any solidarity and sympathy as an alliance of expediency between partners of equal strength and any humanity only as a humanity of expediency. A repentance of this sort, which extends down to the affective foundations of life, is required of us not by some abstract progress of humanity, but by the Church as a eucharistic community and as a sign of messianic hope.

A Brazilian bishop—and it wasn't Dom Helder Camara!—recently wrote to me, 'No German can say he isn't an exploiter'. A hard saying, but nevertheless an episcopal one. We Christians in this country must live with the suspicion of being oppressors, if perhaps oppressed oppressors. The suspicion is not refuted by the fact of our willingness to give alms. The challenges of the love demanded here cannot be satisfied just by the 'sacrament of money', in particular because the way in which that money was acquired itself increases the poverty which the same money is supposed to relieve. Clearly something more is required here, a radical process of repentance, a new relationship, one which is indeed very hard to establish, to social identity, property and affluence in general.

7. SOME RETHINKING

WHERE SHOULD THE CHANGE OF HEART WE HAVE DESCRIBED START?

Where must we begin the change in priorities and the new approaches? It can obviously only be done in lengthy processes of transformation. I am quite certain that there are sufficient reserves of enthusiasm and energy for change even in our Church, but I venture to ask whether these energies are being properly approached and 'harnessed'. For example, do the Church organisations, which are more or less all organised according to social models of a past age, release the spiritual and social energies which are undoubtedly invested in them in a way which allows them to respond to the challenge? Or, to put the question more sharply the other way round, why do the Church authorities want organisations of this type, and why were the new-style youth organisations of the 'sixties treated by the bishops with so much suspicion? Or, to take up an earlier idea, could not the big Church charities, which are almost our only channel for showing solidarity with the poor churches, do much more than just collect money? Ought they not, precisely because they realise that money is far from innocent, take an active part in developing the awareness, not just of the recipient countries, but also particularly of the givers? In this respect I feel that these important charities, as part of a process of universal solidarity, are only in their beginnings.

There are signs that the Christians in West Germany are ready to learn and change. In recent years a hostility, still perhaps rather vague, towards the destructive effects of capitalism has developed at the base. Ecological responsibility is becoming an issue. There is a committed, if still relatively powerless, interest in the plight of the poor churches and of the Third World in general. At the Würzburg synod there was a new attempt, at least at the level of planning, to take up the battle for youth and, no less important, for the workers. If our general pastoral approach turns away from the defeatist attitude of a 'floodgates strategy' and faces the challenges of radical repentance, the beginnings of a new sort of parochial activity, youth work or industrial mission would not have to be given up as lost before they had seriously begun.

When I mentioned signs of a new messianic practice I did not mean just the process in this country which could be called a 'swing to religion' or 'the return of society to religion'. These are popular labels, and recently not only Church circles but also political parties have been trying to cope with this phenomenon, but in my view it is profoundly ambiguous. The 'return to religion' does not necessarily mean that a society, as it were, wants to go beyond itself; it may be calling in religion to enable it to remain itself, to reinforce its own security, because it scents that religion will be its ally in defending a threatened status quo. Where Christianity in this country gives way to this social pressure, it may become more respectable, but I am afraid it also slips even further into the role of a purely ' "bourgeois" religion', soothing society's conscience in the face of the worldwide challenges we have mentioned and enabling it to go on living as it does now. An authentic turning to religion, on the other hand, would have to mean a turning to repentance, to the messianic practice of love.

8. DISCIPLESHIP AS CLASS TREASON?

It is possible that the demands of love here may look like treason—a betrayal of affluence, the family and the customary patterns of life. But it is also possible that this is just the place where we need discernment of spirits in the churches of the rich and powerful countries of this earth. Certainly, Christianity does not exist just for the brave, but we are not the ones who define the challenges of love, and we are not the ones who fix the conditions by which it is tested. So, for example, Christian love in periods of nationalism must be quite prepared to be suspected of lacking national feeling. In situations of racism it will incur the suspicion of race treason. And in periods when the social contradictions in the world cry to heaven it will incur the suspicion of class treason for betraying the allegedly obvious interests of the propertied.

Did not Jesus Himself incur the reproach of treason? Did not His love bring Him to that state? Was He not crucified as a traitor to all the apparently worthwhile values? Must not Christians therefore expect, if they want to be faithful to Him, to Christ, to be regarded as traitors to 'bourgeois' religion? True, His love, in which in the end everything was taken from Him, even all the authority and dignity belonging to love suffering in powerlessness, was still something other than the expression of a sharing in solidarity of the suffering of the unfortunate and oppressed. It was the expression of His obedience, with which He suffered for God and His powerlessness in our world. But must not Christian love, which imitates His, constantly strive towards that obedience?

When the practice of Christian love is placed under the sign of this obedience, which forbids us to confuse the mystery of God's will with the quite unmysterious desire of familiar ways of life for self-preservation, something of the messianic power of this love may be revealed. It strikes deep into preconceived patterns and priorities of life. It has power to move hearts, power not to increase sufferings but to take them on itself. It has the power to show unconditional solidarity, partisan and yet without the destructive hate which negates the individual, combining in itself the aims of sanctity and militant love—even to the folly of the cross. Yes, folly, for such a 'change of hearts' will probably be dismissed by the experienced strategists of the class struggle as feeble or useless, and branded as treason by those who are infatuated with exchange and who reject the inhuman consequences of capitalism only verbally, if at all.

All this may seem to some a considerable exaggeration. But what would a more cautious and 'balanced' discussion of the messianic practice of discipleship be like? And how would caution and 'balance' throw light on the crisis we have been talking about?

Translated by Francis McDonagh

Note

¹ This is a revised version of the lecture I gave to the 1978 Catholic Congress in Freiburg under the title 'Faith—the capacity for a future?' ('Glaube-Befähigung zur Zukunft?'). The emotion which I was both unable and unwilling to remove from the text is perhaps best explained by the fact that in a country in which Christianity, so to say, has a potential majority in political and social life critical attitudes can only be introduced in a more or less 'missionary' speech.

This paper could not deal with many important matters, such as the historical process of the association of Christianity and the 'bourgeoisie' and the so-called dialectic of the 'bourgeois' history of freedom. This is frequently ignored, particularly in progressive liberal theologies, which allows a tacit identification of the 'bourgeois' and the Christian subject. There was also no discussion of the 'bourgeois' principle of individuation and the Christian principle of individuation, etc. For these and similar matters the reader is referred to J. B. Metz *Glaube in Geschichte und Gesellschaft* (2nd ed. 1978).

Dietor Schellong

A Theological Critique
of the 'Bourgeois World-View'
(*Bürgerlichen and Weltanschauung*)

IN THE thought of *Karl Barth* theology appears as a critique of the 'bourgeois world-view' for the first time in recent theological history. Why and in what sense is this the case? Barth deems it a 'bourgeois' treatment of revelation that man takes the Gospel of God under his own direction, that he utilises it for the benefit of his human requirements, regulations and plans and as a means of achieving his self-preservation and self-defence. The 'bourgeois man' endorses what the God of the biblical revelation says to him as if it were his own possibility, 'as a matter for consideration, which he can accept, but of which he is fundamentally the master, which does not cause him any inconvenience, indeed in the possession of which he is doubly secure, justified and rich'.[1] In this enterprise man takes possession of the Gospel and disposes of God's revelation in accordance with his own wishes. This is what Barth terms 'natural theology'.

'Natural theology', as Barth understands it, is by no means bound to adopt an anti-Christian or anti-ecclesiastical posture, for it seldom resorts to direct opposition to the Bible and the Church. As a rule—and this is uppermost in Barth's mind—natural theology is an ingredient of church life, for the Christian faith itself usually lives in a 'bourgeois' manner. By this we mean that it lives in such a way that the believer usurps the truth of God in his own interest. When it draws attention to the peril inherent in such a natural theology, theology furnishes a critique of the 'bourgeois world-view'. This occurs when, without regard for the wishes of the 'bourgeois man', theology demonstrates that the Gospel of Jesus Christ encounters us as something highly alien, and that the message of the

74

Crucified is a joyful message for us only because it judges us and ushers us into a crisis.

With these remarks I have made some allusion to the 'bourgeois world-view' and to the Christian critique that has been levelled against it. This must now be explained and developed. Should what follows sound rather primitive, then it is to be borne in mind that the matter in hand is itself something primitive or, to put it better, something elementary. This elementary matter often unfolds in a very complicated way; so it is difficult (but also necessary) for us to grasp the vital point.[2] I use the expression 'world-view' (*Weltanschauung*) here because I can find no more apposite concept in terms of which it is possible to summarise the convictions and intention of the 'bourgeoisie'. It is not primarily a question of philosophy or even of theology, but of a basic outlook which is at once practical and theoretical.

The crucial characteristic of the 'bourgeoisie' Barth discerned to be the desire to possess or, more precisely, the desire to possess more. All that counts is what we 'have'. The level of our income and the amount of money we have at our disposal determine to which social stratum we belong. With the aid of money we acquire things and status symbols with which we can prove that we belong at least to the middle if not indeed to the upper class. Therefore buying is so important for the 'bourgeois man', and hence continually to be bringing 'yet more' into his own possession. For this reason it is so important for him to pursue a way of life which proves that he has something and that he is in a position to acquire more.

It is also entirely possible for so-called intellectual commodities to be lumped together with property and status symbols. In Europe there is an 'academic middle class', a social stratum whose material standard of living was for a long time nothing to write home about. They participated in the bourgeois way of life, however, by dint of possessing so-called intellectual commodities and by publicly cultivating and augmenting *this* property. In the meantime, of course, it has come about that even among the ranks of the academic middle class the cultivation of educational commodities is not meant to take the place of the inferior material property but only to supplement it. Loss of independence is on the increase in the educational system too, so it seems an obvious step to strive after compensation through the acquisition of material goods. Moreover, those who practise theology largely stem from the academic middle class, at any rate in the sphere of Protestant theology. And theology is everywhere carried on specifically for academic middle class people. I exempt neither myself nor this article from the scope of this observation.

Now it must be observed that the basis of bourgeois existence is modern industry in its distinctively capitalist form. The principal agents of industrial production are the owners of the means of production, who at the present time are often shareholders in large firms. The major consideration in production is the constant raising of dividend returns. This is the chief factor in the treatment of all questions bound up with industrial production, such as the number of jobs, the task of scientific research and so on. The class which, on account of its ownership of the means of production, is concerned with increasing profits through production, is called the 'bourgeoisie'. It is in terms of its principle of life and action that we are to understand what we call 'bourgeois'. This has become the decisive principle and maxim in life for the middle class too, and is identical with having and desiring to have more.

This principle is no secret and is often accorded an explicit public defence as an alleged aspect of personal freedom. The reason offered for this view is that man only works well and satisfactorily when there is a prospect of personal gain. But there is a further cluster of *moral values* which have been associated with this principle. These endow the capitalist way of life with a veneer of moral propriety and are meant at once to veil and to legitimise its principle from a supposedly loftier perspective. This is bound up with two factors. First, the 'bourgeois' principle is intrinsically destructive, for it turns men into competitors and it undermines collective activity. In order to make human fellowship possible and to furnish motives for collective activity notwithstanding this principle, it appears necessary that certain moral values be recognised whose function would be to set limits to competitive behaviour and to bind men to a fellowship valid despite the 'bourgeois' principle.

Secondly, intensive modern industrial production requires institutions to offer men guidance in technological and other knowledge and to furnish them with a training in 'bourgeois' principles and an introduction to the practical side of 'bourgeois' life. These institutions ostracise unsuitable persons and determine the ground rules for this process as well. Last but not least they buttress and canalise commerce and guarantee industrial expansion from the perspective of high finance and power politics. In this way the 'bourgeoisie' has created a series of institutions which characterise 'bourgeois' society and which promote and stabilise industrial production to the extent laid down by the pursuit of the maximum private profit for the benefit of the owners of the means of production. Chief among such institutions is the State which, under the domination of the 'bourgeoisie', has become something significantly different from all that hitherto went by the name of 'State'. To the institutions that I have in mind belong all kinds of schools and the armed forces; moreover, I wish to make mention of hospitals, in particular those for people certified as mentally ill, and of prisons. The State is at once the promoter of private enterprise and the principal organiser of all the institutions I have mentioned; and it is these things pre-eminently in its role as nation-state.

The moral values of the 'bourgeoisie' attach themselves primarily to this State and serve as a means to achieve men's commitment to nation and State. And it is from the perspective of these values that justification is given for the various individual institutions. The higher totality, which allegedly adds up to more than just the competitive struggle for the highest profit, is represented in the nation, the State and the institutions proper to them. The moral values of the 'bourgeoisie' are inseparably bound up with the realities of the organisations of the 'bourgeois' State, for moral values are devoid of vigour when they are not represented by institutional realities.

Natural theology conscripts the revelation of God in Jesus Christ to help achieve moral commitment to the nation and the State; and it uses it to provide a sacral guarantee for the individual institutions I have mentioned. Therefore there are chaplains to the armed forces, prisons and hospitals; and there is for the same reason an intimate fusion of school and Church, hospital and Church, etc. So the desire to possess and to exploit seizes control of the Gospel too. It would be the special task of a theology which saw itself as a critique of the 'bourgeois world-view' to criticise and dissolve this symbiosis of profit, the State and the institutions and morality that accompany it, and the Christian faith. It would also be obliged to speak of the biblical God in such a way that it becomes clear that this God has nothing to do with this whole syncretistic business, and that at any rate he does not exist as a mere prop of human organisations. For Christ did not come as a servant of our 'bourgeois' life, and the Kingdom of Christ, the Crucified and Risen One, is not of this world.

This means that symbols of nation and State, such as flags, have nothing to do with the revelation of the biblical God. The whole Christian-religious fuss made over flags, uniforms and courts of law is theologically insufferable. The 'socialist States' do without the Christian consecration of these institutions and have developed a world-view of their own along with their own rites for the glorification of these things. This is certainly thoroughly pagan, but it is less offensive to a critical Christian theology because it dispenses with the exploitation of Christian truth in the service of State institutions.

Certainly the fact that the 'socialist States' have taken over and in doing so have strengthened rather than weakened, all the 'bourgeois' institutions and organisations I have mentioned, is of interest and provides food for thought. The 'bourgeoisie' has evidently stamped the modern world so distinctly that even its opponents can do no other than work with its models. But can the same means be used to build a *different* society? This is an open question, which must be posed with some scepticism. We cannot deal with it more closely here, and I only mention it for the sake of completeness. Here we have to direct our attention to the ordering of life in 'bourgeois' society, something that is carried out through a veritable plethora of organisations. So accustomed are we to this that we can no longer imagine a life devoid of all those organisations such as the school, the armed forces and so on; and we readily accept it when ever more money, time and effort are put into them and they swell into a Moloch which is threatening to swallow us all up. To us this seems 'natural', so natural that we do not even have a name for these far-reaching organisations! Nor do I know what we should call them; so I use alternately the concepts *Einrichtung* (institution), *Veranstaltung* (organisation) and *Institution*. Indeed, so natural do these organisations seem to us that we do not notice the changes that they are continually undergoing or how they are the principal instruments in a strategy of power in whose sight most of their admirers are mere objects. We do not notice this because we identify ourselves with these organisations, and our minds are completely befuddled by the use of the Christian tradition to achieve this identification.[3]

It was a deliberate choice of words on my part to say that these institutions strike us as 'natural', for it is a major element in the 'bourgeois' world-view to look upon what is 'bourgeois' as 'natural'. The pursuit of profit and competition, the nation, the school and the armed forces, and even the Christian transfiguration of these things are all deemed 'natural' by the bourgeois man. In this way they find their sanction, and therefore everyone in whose eyes some aspects of them are questionable appears to be a fool. And the Christian doctrine of creation can be made to serve as a buttress of the right of the 'natural', whereby it is presupposed that such things as we have been talking about are identical with what is 'natural'.

And since all this seems to be 'natural', there can also be confidence concerning the outcome of the historical process. After all, does not 'Nature' help itself? Is it not 'natural' that life is only developed in the element of competitive struggle? Indeed, is it not always developed onto a higher plane in the process? The notion of evolution is the decisive and central ideological concept with whose aid the 'bourgeoisie' interprets its own history. Even the support of Christian eschatology can be enlisted in the prosecution of this cause, for in the end of the day revelation gives man the hope that God will also preserve and bring to a goodly end what he has created. Thus elements of Christian truth can apparently be brought into a seemly union with the fundamental principles of the 'bourgeois' world-view. The work of 'natural theology' is precisely this.

But in this case appearances are deceptive, and if we consider this alliance a genuine one then we must be deceiving ourselves on two levels, namely that of reality and that of Christian truth. First of all, let us deal with hard reality. For it pertains to the 'bourgeois' world-view to over-look the ravages and devastation wrought by the principle of profit and competition. Even when these are perceived they are interpreted as the necessary reverse side of the coin of progress which need disturb us no further. I need only recall the sacrifices that have been made to indus-trialisation: to begin with there was the impoverished proletariat, and at the present day there is the environment, not to mention living conditions in general. Let us remind ourselves in addition of the elimination of the original population of America and of the monstrous measures of exploi-tation and destruction carried out in the Colonies.

These facts, which in the last analysis we can no longer suppress, are endowed with erroneous names and assigned bogus causes. Thus the former colonies are now called 'developing countries', although this term refers not simply to undeveloped cultures but to cultures that have been destroyed by Western exploitation. That something that has been des-troyed can be termed 'undeveloped' by those who have destroyed it, is an example of dishonest use of language. This lack of honesty is all the more galling in that the 'developing countries' are still largely obliged to be geared to the requirements of the rich peoples, being therefore unable to develop in accordance with their own needs. As an example of an errone-ous statement of cause let us mention the thesis of overpopulation. Already in the nineteenth century Malthus attributed the misery of the proletariat to their excessive numbers. He was justly contradicted by Marx, who explained that human misery is a consequence of wrongful patterns of ownership and evil social structures. This is being repeated today on a global scale.[4]

A Christian orientation can acquiesce neither in these lies nor in the resigned toleration of unspeakable sacrifices. It would have to overcome the 'bourgeois' indifference to everything apart from private gain and prestige. To do this, however, it would have to extricate itself from the stranglehold of the 'bourgeois' world-view.

My second point concerns truthfulness in the face of what the reve-lation of God in Jesus Christ says to us. 'Bourgeois' optimism and the 'bourgeoisie's' idea of what is 'natural' are contrary to Christian truth. This means that we deceive ourselves about the Christian revelation should we wish to exploit it in the interests of the 'bourgeois' world-view.

For the fact is that there is nothing 'natural' which we should not have to see in the light of the Cross and Resurrection of Jesus Christ. What does this mean? That Jesus Christ was crucified, shows us that God and ourselves do not live in harmony. In the Crucifixion there takes place the expulsion and brutal removal of God when He draws too close to us, when in His son He draws so close to us that it is no longer possible for us to fashion an image of Him convenient to ourselves and capable of being used in accordance with our own desires. And it is precisely the 'builders' who have rejected the 'cornerstone' (Ps. 118:22), precisely the responsible and pious folk who slay Him, thereby bringing to light the truth of the relationship all of us have with God. This relationship is profoundly marked by human sin, and we can fall back upon no 'natural' harmony that lies behind it. By means of the Cross, then, our true condition is made manifest. And because the Word of the Cross sets this truth before our eyes, it arouses offence to this day.

At the same time, however, the Word of the Cross (1 Cor. 1:18 ff) is God's message of deliverance. For God did not draw near to us only in order that our sins should be exposed. For Him there is something positive involved, namely that He rescue us from sin, reconcile us with Himself and overcome our aggressive hostility by His humility. Our being confronted with our sin occurs as the reverse side of God's cancellation of sin. This positive event does not take place through any work of ours, but through God's act of humility shown in delivering his Son to the Cross.

It is important that both our sin and God's act of salvation be looked at in conjunction with one another. Even so, the endeavour is often made to defend the 'bourgeois' behaviour described above with the help of an alleged insight into human sinfulness. For a change this is not undertaken on the basis of an 'unimpaired nature' but with the argument that men are bad. As sinners they could not do other than be driven by the desire to have more, and so in this state they would perceive themselves as rivals. With respect to this truth about the human condition capitalism is alleged to be the appropriate system and therefore legitimate. But God does not show us the extent of our sinful decay so that we can capitalise on it and use it to justify our selfishness. Sin can only be examined in shame and dismay and in thankful acceptance of the fact that God has not only uncovered but also overcome it in Jesus' death on the Cross, and that in this death He has turned us to Himself. Thus we cannot acquiesce in sin. On the contrary insight into our sin propels us towards conversion and practical change.

All this has become clear in God's raising of the Crucified. Because of this the positive aspect prevails—not anything positive that *we* are or set in motion, but the positive element present in the divine act of the sacrifice of the Son of God. So the victor is not human wickedness but God, namely, the God who loves us and suffers with and for us. The revelation of God does not nail us immutably to our sin, but shows how God has broken through our sin, by way of self-sacrifice and humility, with the upshot that a way is opened up into the realm of freedom.

Some closing suggestions:

(a) That it is the Resurrection of Jesus from the dead in which God's activity for us culminates, shows how immense is the revolutionary change of which the Christian revelation speaks and how little we can lay claim to divine approbation of our life as it actually is. The God of the Resurrection, the Father of the Crucified One who has been raised up, does not affirm our everyday way of going about things, he denies it. He promises a completely new world. This is the precise meaning of Cross and Resurrection. This God does not stand at the beck and call of the 'bourgeois' world-view, nor can we exploit Him as a means to this end.

(*b*) It will be asked whether this is valid only with reference to the 'bourgeois world-view'. Is only the *bourgeois* man brought into a *crisis* when he encounters God's revelation? Or would not what we have said be bound to apply to every man? Karl Barth indeed meant it in just this way, for in 'bourgeois' man he saw the typical man. Thus every man encounters God with a view to exploiting Him and, if He cannot be exploited, of doing Him harm.

But is there then any point in dubbing this activity of man 'bourgeois' and in using the specialist word 'bourgeois' to express this universal phenomenon? There is sense in this choice of words, for we are then calling something concrete by name. In this way we recognise that our existence before God also has a distinct worldly form. How we should prefer to leave this fact in obscurity! How we should prefer so to shunt our sin into the realm of inwardness so that nothing definite can be linked with it, and that nothing definite flows from it with reference to the way we run our lives! If in other periods the discord between man and God took on a different outward form, in the modern age it is the 'bourgeoisie' that is moulding world history and that is causing man's discord with God to adopt a particular worldly form.

(*c*) What flows from this perception? Many may think that we must read a practicable prescription out of the revelation of God which would dictate how we are to conduct ourselves with a view to the amelioration of social conditions and patterns of behaviour. But this opinion is merely a further manifestation of the capitalist impulse to exploit everything, even God's revelation. What is at stake is that we should let ourselves be led by God into the *crisis* He has prepared, and that the insights mentioned in this article should begin by taking a breather. In this process it will come about that the sacrifices made to the desire to have more will no longer leave us coldly indifferent. Nor shall we go on passively accepting intellectual obscurations of our real life and of God's revelation. And we shall seek fellowship with persons who adopt a critical stance *vis-à-vis* the life-style that goes along with a continuous increase in material possessions. All this is not without importance for our daily lives if the Crucified One unites us to Himself. When this happens the result will be solidarity with men who exist on the shady and dubious side of reality; but in expressing this solidarity we shall not be able to act as if *we* were the creators of a new world.

We are thus brought to the question of our *freedom*. Everything to which I have referred in this article could also be expressed in a treatment of the concept of freedom. Or, to put it better, it would require to be developed further in that direction. The concrete critique of the 'bourgeois world-view' must probably be carried out in the dispute about the true idea of freedom. Even so, this cannot be accomplished in few words and must therefore be omitted on this occasion.[5]

Translated by John Stephenson

Notes

1. Karl Barth *Kirchliche Dogmatik* (Zollikon and Zürich 1960) II/1, p. 156; (Church Dogmatics II/1. p. 141).

2. I have endeavoured to do this in greater detail in the pamphlet 'Bürgertum und christliche Religion' (Munich 1975) (*Theologische Existenz heute* 187).

3. It is the merit of Michel Foucault's brilliant work, *Surveiller et punir. La naissance de la prison* (Paris 1975), to have pioneered an intellectual approach to this whole complex of problems.

4. We should take note of Joseph Collins/France Moore Lappé *Food first— Beyond the Myth of Scarcity* (Institute for Food and Development Policy, San Francisco 1977).

5. For some first tentative steps in that direction, see my essay 'Karl Barth als Theologe der Neuzeit' in K. D. Steck/D. Schellong *Karl Barth und die Neuzeit* (Munich 1973) (*Theologische Existenz heute* 173).

Arthur I. Waskow

Toward a Jewish Theology of the Middle Class

THE DEVELOPMENT of a Jewish theology of the modern 'middle class' would rest on certain basic approaches, methods, and assumptions:

1. That in this period of history, the world and the Jewish people have undergone an earthquake of 'modernity' as powerful as the earthquake of Helleno-Roman conquest that transformed the world and the Jewish people about 2000 years ago. In that era, the Jewish response was a renewed wrestle with the texts of Torah in the light of new social conditions, and the result was the creation of the Talmud. In our era, especially after the earthquakes of the holocaust, the creation of the State of Israel, and the emergence of an unprecedentedly free and politically powerful Diaspora in the United States, it is necessary to renew an equally profound process of wrestling with the original texts of the tradition—both Biblical and Talmudic.

2. That the traditional midrashic process by which a Jewish community standing authentically in its own life re-examines the Tradition and rediscovers within it a teaching of how to live Jewishly is the process to be applied in achieving new theological insights and new life-practices.

3. That just as Jacob wrestled 'with men and with God' to become Israel, the God-wrestler, so the midrashic process requires a wrestling not only with texts but with human beings and the social system. Midrash flows not from the ivory tower but from the sweat, dust and struggle.

In accordance with this process, I propose that a useful beginning-point for a modern Jewish theology of economics, class, and an understanding of the relationship of the human race to the world environment (now profoundly intertwined with economic questions) is the Biblical tradition of the Jubilee.

I suggest this as the starting-point on the ground that the present economic/environmental situation of the industrial nations is one in which the past 300 years of explosive economic 'development' in a dominantly economistic fashion, undermining the values of community, personhood, and the integrity of the natural world, have reached the frontier of disaster. The exemplar of this process in the world today is the United States, but Western Europe, Japan and the Soviet Union have pursued basically the same path.

During the past generation, this approach has run head-on into four limiting factors:

1. It had integrated more and more of the world, especially the southern hemisphere, into the northern industrial corporate or state-bureacratic spheres of political and economic control—but now the resistance to such economic domination and privilege has grown quite strong.

2. It had resorted to enormous military spending as both an economic crutch and a technique for managing foreign political opposition; but the military system has become intrinsically dangerous and internally de-stabilising.

3. It had subjected large realms of the natural world to its immediate economic needs; but this environmental control has become self-destructive as both the depletion of natural resources and the poisoning of the environment by waste products have accelerated.

4. It had created new mass media as means of holding the society together spiritually and psychologically—but the internal dynamics of these media have driven them into using more and more violence, sex, hyper-acquisitive and hyper-competitive games so that the media themselves have become increasingly dangerous to the senses of community, trust, and repose on which any coherent society must ground itself.

On the contrary, the Jubilee tradition (Leviticus 25) is based on expectations and desires of a 'pulsating' rather than 'exploding' economy, and bears the imprint of a culture quite different from that of swift economic development.

The Jubilee requires that:

(a) In every seventh year, the land lie fallow and all debts be annulled.

(b) In every fiftieth year (the year after the seventh seventh year) the land lie fallow again and every family receive back the allotment of land that it had originally received. The rich give up their surplus and the poor receive their due. All slaves and indentured servants—even those who are in the middle of a seven-year term of servitude or who have voluntarily chosen life-long slavery—go free.

Most profoundly, perhaps, the Jubilee insists that 'religious' and 'spiritual' questions cannot be separated from 'political' or 'economic' issues. Indeed, such language is itself inadequate to express the Jubilee's rooted intertwining of what we now see as separate domains of life that must with great effort be brought together. For the Jubilee says that *at the same moment* everyone receives land to work, and everyone rests from working the land. *At the same moment*—the rich give up their surplus, the poor get back their share—and the whole society gives up the land to God. *At the same moment* there is what Marxism demands—that everyone be equal in economic base so as to be equal in freedom and power; and what Buddhism demands—that everyone not-do and not-own, so as to be in touch with spiritual truth.

The Jubilee tradition says to us, You cannot achieve either 'Marxism' or 'Buddhism' alone. It says, There is no way to achieve spiritual transcendence, no way to renounce material values, unless you know that everyone needs and must share the wealth.

Moreover, the Jubilee speaks about a cycle of change. It does not imagine that the land can be shared and justice achieved once and for all; and it does not imagine that a little change, year after year, can make for real justice. The Jubilee says that in every year the poor must be allowed to glean in the corners of the field, that in every seventh year loans must be forgiven and the poor lifted from the desperation of debt; but that once in every generation there must be a great transformation—and that each generation must know it will have to be done again, in the next generation.

So the Jubilee seems to be saying that we know full well that some are capable and some are schlemiehls, some are greedy and some are modest, some are frenetic and some are lazy, some are lucky and some are schimazls. So some will become rich and others become poor, and this is all right!—so long as there is a corrective, so long as the society can remake itself and start over again. This rhythm is not what we have come to know as conservative or liberal or radical. It carries a more cunning sense of human behaviour than any one of them.

And the Jubilee says that there is a connection between the cycle of nature and the cycle of human life. First of all, the Jubilee is rooted in a set of smaller rhythms:

On the seventh day, on Shabbos, there is a mini-Jubilee: no one works, everyone shares.

In every seventh month (the seventh month of Tishri, in the fall, and the seventh month of Nisan, in the spring), there is a holy festival; Rosh Hashana, Yom Kippur, and Sukkos in the fall; Passover in the spring. Days of rest, renewal, sharing—sharing the frail hut of the Sukkah, sharing the flat bread of the matzah.

In every seventh year all debts are forgiven and the land lies fallow.

Then, the rhythm whirls up the final spiral to the Jubilee. So the sense of the grand social cycle would have been inescapable each Sabbath—faint perhaps but inescapable on each small weekly cycle.

And how does the cycle feel when the Jubilee itself comes round at last? There stands the land untilled as it stood the year before, the seventh seventh year. Two years in a row untilled! Imagine standing in the midst of a farming society where twice in a row the land had gone unsown, the trees and vines unpruned. Where the free growth of the soil was for every family to pluck, not for the owners to harvest systematically. Imagine how strange the land would look: more than a touch of wilderness, a fifth 'season' of the year. Nature itself would be transformed along with the society; everyone would have a sense that doing something so basic as sharing the wealth could change something so basic as how the plants grew. Everyone would learn that the 'biggest' action of all was to not act.

Further, let us try to imagine the farmer who stands on his family plot of land, thinking to himself: here, right here, is where my grandparents stood fifty years ago, and here, right here, is where my grandchildren will stand fifty years hence. No matter what happens—there may be a drought and my children move to the city or sell themselves into slavery; there may be a plenitude and they come to own half Judaea; but come what may, in fifty years here my seed will stand, knowing *this* hill and *this* well-spring, *this* rock and *this* olive tree.

Between the renewed health of my small family and the renewed health of my whole country, land and people, there is a clear unity. For it is only in the restoration of each family that our country is restored: no king, no priest is responsible to do this renewal. Only my family—and every other family.

All this is not what we learn from modern secular politics. Today conservatives who demand that the family be strengthened turn furious at the idea of abolishing all wealth and privilege. Radicals who demand that the rich be expropriated are baffled at the ideas that the land should be left unproductive, or the regressive institution of the family be celebrated.

The Jubilee also stands beyond both the 'moral' politics of middle-class guilt toward the poor and the politics of the class-interest of the poor themselves. Its point of reference is simply not the poor, either as the actors themselves, or as the focus of action by others. The image of the Jubilee is not that a great mass of the poor and desperate, the wretched of the earth and the prisoners of starvation, arise in rage to take back the land from the swollen rich. Nor is it that the affluent renounce their wealth in a fit of guilt or pity. Indeed, one aspect of the Jubilee suggests that rage and guilt are both to be excluded from its motives; for the Jubilee Year begins not at Rosh Hashanah when the fiftieth year itself begins, but ten days later—on Yom Kippur, when the community has already purged itself of guilt and rage. When the Days of Awe and Turning have already accomplished atonement, the Jubilee is proclaimed. Thus it is both the final healing gift of the people to God to complete the old cycle, and God's first blessing to the people in the new cycle.

The Jubilee incorporates both the sense of concern for the other that infuses a religious-humanist politics, and the sense of class interest and solidarity that infuses a politics of conflict. Instead of proclaiming hatred for the rich, it offers a 'release' for the rich as well as the poor. The rich are released from working, bossing, increasing production—and from others' envy of them. The poor are released from working, from hunger, from humiliation and despair, from dependence on charity or even on the righteousness of others—from others' pity of them. They are given the wherewithal to work again. Both the rich and the poor are seen as fully human, as counterparts to be encountered—not as enemies or victims to be feared and hated.

But the Jubilee was not based only on the recognition of God's image in every human being. It may very well have appealed to the class interests of a large group of independent small farmers who wanted to prevent the emergence of a permanent, ever-fattening class of large landholders on the one hand and a class of permanent slaves or debtors who would undercut their incomes, on the other.

So let us imagine that the Jubilee could nowadays become not a model but a pointer, an indicator. A pointer to what the middling classes could say in the search for a decent society—beyond their own greed, beyond their own guilt.

Imagine the Jubilee applied to the despair, violence, anomie, alienation of modern cities. Applied to drug abuse, the disintegration of families, violence not only on the streets but within families, the abuse of children, the abandonment of old people. What would it say?

That everyone must know *for sure* that neither poverty nor charity will last forever . . . that decent work, a decent economic independence, is coming to everyone. That there must be hope—not the hope of fantasy, but the hope of sure knowledge. That hope is both spiritual and economic. That in one's own locality, in one's own community, not in the cosmopolitan clatter of tongues, is where not only cultural roots but sturdy economic independence must be grown.

That the community must honour the cycles of life—plant, animal and human life. The cycle of the seasons and of the generations. That individual rest is not enough. That whole communities must take rest together for that rest to be truly refreshing. That just as communal rest is necessary for the renewal of work, a rhythm of communal return to the songs, stories, crafts, and foods of communal roots is necessary to healthy cultural growth. That a rhythmical communal celebration of earth and air and water is necessary for a healthy return to the rush of contact with other human beings. That we must find some way to recreate the rhythms of rest, roots and nature—to recreate these rhythms in the very midst of the cities where they are now abandoned.

That the 'middle class' must see itself, and remake itself, as co-operative co-owners of and co-workers in the means of production. In many industrial societies, large parts of the 'middle class' have become manipulators of large-scale structures of domination and dependency in the guise of social welfare. Thus there are now often counted among the middle class social workers, who are hired to manage, assist, and control the poor, sick, unemployed and helpless; teachers, who are hired to control and channel the young into various groupings of technical, manual, and other skilled labour and the arena of the unemployable; media workers, hired to reduce the mental independence and alertness of the public; etc., etc.

Two generations ago, the left wing of the Zionist movement spoke (in secular socialist rather than religious language) of the special danger of this new and parasitic form of the middle class to the Jewish community. As Ber Borochov explained, the traditional assignment of Jews in Christian Europe to pariah status made it easy to place Jews in the marginal positions of overseeing the poor and the peasantry while holding no real power of their own. The left Zionist solution to this problem was the reconstitution of the Jewish people as a self-governing working-class people on its own land, the land of Israel. The collective ownership of land, as developed by kibbutzim and the Jewish Agency, was an attempt to restore a 'middling' class, neither rich nor poor, neither property-less workers nor propertied capitalists, as the heart of a renewed Jewish peoplehood. The Borochov/kibbutz analysis therefore distinguished between the conventional 'middle' class of marginal business people and marginal welfare bureaucrats, and a new kind of 'middling' class— perhaps best seen as a translation into modern terms of the independent agricultural yeomanry.

Drawing on the lessons of this secular experiment, and deepening its insights by drawing on the religious tradition, we might suggest the following new elements:

That the Jewish communities in the Diaspora might extend this distinction to the Diaspora itself and to the non-Jewish groupings that have replaced or joined Jews in the welfarist 'middle' class (subject to hostility from both the poor and the ruling class). The reconstruction of the conventional middle class into a new, self-determining 'middling' class need not be restricted to the Land of Israel. Within the northern industrial societies, Jews and non Jews might both learn to apply the basic teachings of the Jubilee and the experience of the kibbutz.

That the respect for the land itself and for all of God's world-environment that are mandated by the Jubilee should be applied in ways that secularist socialists have usually not required.

That the importance of communal rest, repose, and re-rooting and of the family—also values taught by the Jubilee but not by the secular Left—be entwined with the importance of changes in class structure.

For Judaism (and other religious traditions) to undertake these efforts would require the throwing-off of the pervasive embarrassment that has afflicted all religious thought during the explosive scientific-industrial period of the last 300 years, and an internal decision that Biblical teaching deals profoundly and correctly not only with individual spirituality but also with the broadest economic, political, and environmental issues facing the human collectivity. This task—the internal regeneration and taking-breath—is perhaps the most difficult.

PART III

Controversies

Norbert Schiffers

Soteriology without Christology? Marginal Notes on non-Bourgeois Christologies

BOTH 'BOURGEOIS' (*Bürgerlich*) and 'non-bourgeois' (*nicht-bürgerlich*) are badly defined categories.

From the Marxist point of view a category is meant to show a class's place in productive relationships. But instead of this Marx himself describes merely the attitudes of the 'bourgeois'. The 'petit bourgeois' is 'blinded by the splendour of the higher bourgeoisie and feels compassion for the sufferings of the people'. This does not place the 'petit bourgeois' in a category: instead it describes his attitudes. Its political consequences are that it leads to sniffing out people's views and patterns of thought and judging them on that basis.

Hence when 'non-bourgeois' theologies are mentioned in what follows the qualification should not be understood in a Marxist sense.

Roland Barthes laments that 'bourgeois' ways of thought deny social differences. The object of calculation is the good fortune of equals. The 'bourgeois' pragmatic approach reduces reality to equations. The opportunities for 'bourgeois' are calculated on the basis of social Darwinism in 'bourgeois' thought. The poor do not come into account. 'Non-bourgeois' thought on the other hand is concerned with differences. The inequalities between rich and poor, those who are free and those who are dependent, those who are committed and those who are apathetic are grasped dialectically, and the aim is to overcome them. The model for this process of liberation is provided by Hegel, who makes consciousness like thought become operational. By 'bourgeois' or 'non-bourgeois' are meant categories of the complete process of thought, categories for the consciousness. The formal pattern of thought of 'non-bourgeois' theologies is dialectical. There is no question of Poujardism with regard to the idea of salvation or soteriology. But when soteriologists talk about sinners and those who are justified, then as far as the contents are concerned they already have at the back of their mind the idea of salvation for everyone. Salvation represents a goal, an aim, not a formal category of thought like the dialectic. And when it becomes aware of the presuppositions involved in its contents soteriology adopts a procedure that is not formally dialectical. Barthes' categories—thinking in equations or dialectical thinking—can apply to soteriologists' thought-processes, but not to the salvation of all mankind. The presupposition and the goal of salvation as grace cannot be satisfactorily comprehended within the categories of 'bourgeois' and 'non-bourgeois'.

In censuses in capitalist countries people are assigned to 'bourgeois' occupational groups. Thus in France nine 'bourgeois' occupational groups are listed, of which number 4 includes 'professions and senior management' and number 9 includes 'clergy'.

Those who have worked out the 'non-bourgeois' theologies to be discussed here are professors and can thus be regarded as coming within both these groups. They are therefore 'bourgeois', according to the census classification, as too is the author of these marginal notes. Three considerations therefore need to be borne in mind.

First, as a 'bourgeois' I can only write marginal notes on 'non-bourgeois' theologies: glosses written in the margin by someone whose way of life does not fall within the 'non-bourgeois' occupational groups that 'non-bourgeois' theologies are concerned with.

Second, if 'bourgeois' write as authors of 'non-bourgeois' theologies, they are writing out of a sense of commitment for other people—for example, for the poor. 'Bourgeois' write 'for' the poor when their economic needs are looked after by a religious house or university.

Third, someone who is not living in poverty with the poor, for example in a *communauté de base* in a run-down area, someone who for whatever reason cannot live in such conditions, must, if he is writing a 'non-bourgeois' theology, direct against himself the critique involved in the experiences of the poor, of those in prison, of the oppressed—and thus against what he is writing. Educated 'bourgeois' cannot write 'for' the poor who are unable to articulate their own experience and reflection. Instead of bridging by their writing the gulf of awareness between educated and poor they will rather deepen it. Critical recollection is not simply an attitude but in 'non-bourgeois' theologies is rather a necessity.[1]

1. CHRISTOLOGY WITHOUT SOTERIOLOGY IS A BEAUTIFUL ILLUSION

Before the council of Chalcedon (451) there was dispute within the Church between Christologists moving towards the right and soteriologists moving towards the left.[2] What both parties had in common was a feeling for the injustice to be found in the world. The orthodox reacted with sensitivity to the world's hopeless distress. Human consciousness struck them as like rusting iron: dirty, corroded. Only God's fire could make this consciousness glow again, said the radical orthodox, the fire that without any stain of rust glowed through Jesus' human nature. It was this fire that they wanted to see. They wanted to make God's fire their way of looking at and understanding the world. With the intention of their will the radical Christocentrics of that time did indeed ascribe to Jesus a human body and soul. But they denied him a human spirit, a consciousness that was corroded by contact with the pollution of the world, the filth of the poor. Their aim was to transcend a human consciousness that had become weak in the mysticism of a theosophy, of a wisdom that wants to see only what is divine. Instead of 'spirit and fire' (Origen) they wanted here and now, beyond the history of blood and iron, to see in the shape of Jesus the spirit glowing with the divine fire. Pure Christology, a soteriology that had already reached completion before the eschatological fulfilment, was to be their philosophy.

This vision of the pure ideal was a 'Christology *sans* soteriology'; for soteriology sees what should be in history, not in the hereafter. It does not live in 'bourgeois' fashion on the basis of a beautiful illusion, not even on the basis of the illusion of the shining purity of an ideal Christ. Ideal concepts that do not fit in with the reality of Jesus are of no use.

2. SOTERIOLOGY WITHOUT CHRISTOLOGY IS CROSS-EYED

The 'soteriology moving towards the left' in the early Church found its image of God and of Jesus among the poor. As far as it was concerned Jesus was the Messiah of the poor, in Hebrew for the *ebionim*. For the Ebionites Jesus is close to people. He puts basic human capabilities into practice: loving, liberating, washing dirt from people's wounds, healing, living in solidarity with the poor. His closeness to us comes out too with regard to the image we make for ourselves of God, the father of the poor. The sermon on the mount and the discourse on the last judgement, the accounts of His journeys and miracles are not marginal to the tradition about Christ. According to Matthew (5:19) God's transforming closeness, God's love, already in the Old Testament a commandment for human behaviour, is redeemed by Jesus in action and teaching. This leftwards-inclined Christology rarely considers the accounts of the resurrection. It is concerned rather with the earthly Jesus, the fundamentally human Jesus. The soteriology of the early Church arouses a ready echo. Its theologians lived among the poor. Others worked with their hands. The Bible was something they lived at the rock-bottom of society. They experienced life and they reflected on what they experienced. Their soteriology, their teaching about the salvation brought by Jesus was practical, full of hope, committed.

But one question remains unsettled: if Christians can do what Christ Jesus did, where is there a difference between Christ and Christians? If for their active discipleship Christians have need of the examplar of Christ, what does this mean other than that the consciousness of Christians is weak and that of Christ alone is divine and strong? The soteriologists of the early Church must let Christocentrics tell them: 'With one eye you are looking at Christ in his strength and with the other you are looking at the people of the poor. You are not seeing straight. You are cross-eyed.' According to Marx this would be 'bourgeois'.

3. ON CHALCEDON: TWICE YES AND ONCE NO

The aim of the council of Chalcedon was to put an end to the dispute. The cardinal point at issue in the dispute had meanwhile become clear. Those on the right said Jesus had only a divine consciousness, while those on the left insisted that Jesus had shown a human consciousness. The council decided that Jesus Christ had both, a divine as well as a human consciousness. There was no separation or division, as the Christocentrics thought. Nor was there any confusion or commingling, as was said by the Christians concentrating on discipleship, the followers of a pragmatic left-wing soteriology. Throwing earthly water on to divine fire generates steam, not spirit. 'Without confusion or mutability or division or separation' runs the formula of conciliation worked out at Chalcedon (DS 302).

Was this the solution? Yes and no.

Yes: in the formula the council uses a terminology derived from Greek philosophy. To put it more precisely, the terms chosen come from a philosophy which seeks to establish a rational basis for existence. This corresponded to the starting-point that both Christocentrics and soteriologists had in common. Both were asking which consciousness we should be guided by if life in the world, given the world as it is, is to make sense. Today Hans Küng is still asking this kind of question.[3]

Yes: in its formula the council is operating with an idiosyncratic logic. It uses the conjunction 'and' to link two characteristic qualities that are mutually exclusive, like 'without confusion' or 'without separation'. If one wishes to characterise more precisely some object of human earthly experience and thus to use language according to the normal semantic rules, one will say for example of water and wine that nobody has mixed them together and that they are still separate in two separate vessels, or alternatively that someone has mixed them together and that now they are no longer separate. The council's formula, however, 'without confusion or mutability or division or separation', is semantically meaningless. If it is meant to mean something—and after all the council wanted to say something meaningful it cannot mean anything purely earthly. It could however point to a mystery that in some way concerns mankind. The Chalcedonian formula indicates a mystery that to believers in Christ means a great deal, means everything.

No: in order to avoid stating something that could only mean something in the private language games of Christians the council with its terminology went back to a philosophy of being. In being, Greek philosophers had been saying from Heraclitus on, fundamental elements like fire and water did not exclude each other. Nor then did human and divine consciousness exclude each other, especially if being were another name for God. In terms of Greek philosophy this works, or rather, to put it more precisely, it works if this philosophy is orientated towards being and thus in Greek terms has an ontological orientation. It was this orientation to which the fathers of Chalcedon were referring, and on this basis they were able to say what they wanted to say about the mystery of Christ. There was, of course, a high price to be paid, and what this price is is something of which Heidegger has made us aware. We can indeed think our way from being to time, but cannot in reverse infer being from history. The council wanted to talk about the mystery in Jesus Christ. So it used ontological language; and on this lofty plateau of being it missed the lowlands of history formed of blood, poverty, dirt and injustice. The council screened out history, in which the dispute between left-wing and right-wing Christologists over the correct form of consciousness had its context—and still has today.

The ontologically formulated Christology of Chalcedon is, in this formulation, a Christology which is not of practical application in time, and thus in the setting where soteriology makes sense. The Christology of Chalcedon succeeded in neutralising the soteriological aspects that were proper to it. At too high and elevated a level even what is effective for salvation becomes ineffective—in any event for people who are looking for God and His salvation in history.

With its formula Chalcedon provided an answer to the question: 'Who is God and who is man in Jesus Christ? How do they show themselves?' The answer was: 'Jesus Christ has at one and the same time the consciousness of God and the consciousness of man'.

4. JESUS' DEATH SHOWS THAT NOBODY CAN KEEP AN EYE ON GOD

Hans Urs von Balthasar insists on this simultaneity of human and divine consciousness in Jesus Christ. He does admittedly acknowledge the

utmost sensitivity for injustice in the world on the part of nineteenth-
and twentieth-century Christocentrics—English, German, Russian
philosophers of religion with a Christian orientation. He can understand
that Christian theosophy finds the focus of its outlook in the pure and
exclusively divine awareness of Jesus. But to this temptation to a mysticism that transcends time he opposes his large-scale theology of the
'triduum of death'. For someone who does not see that before his resurrection Christ was among the dead, the defeated, the forsaken, God's
light falls not on the history of the defeated but on the isolated victor
Christ.[4]

Jürgen Moltmann concentrates on the event of the cross. Admittedly
he begins by rather naïvely calling Jesus' cross a 'game' in which the loser
wins. But then he says, no longer simply in the formal language of the
dialectic (here the loser wins) but with the seriousness of the Reformation, that the cross reveals 'who and where God is'. This is the Reformation theology of grace. If the Chalcedonian formula was asking 'how'
divine and human consciousness were found together in Christ, then the
question of Reformed Christianity is 'where' God is in whom we human
beings find grace. This is the question of soteriology. Moltmann's answer
is that God is in the cross of Jesus. He is the 'crucified God'. The question
asked by Christians in the presence of Christ, the question of finding a
satisfactory basis for existence in a world of injustice, of incom-
prehensible suffering, of frustrated liberation, has landed once again on
the theologians' desk to demand an answer; and it is not a desk to be
found in heaven or on an earth unredeemed by Jesus' passion. Rather is it
a table at which those who share the meal know that it is between the ages
that they gaze on the cross of Christ in order to experience God's
presence as salvation and thus to act as God acted.[5]

Balthasar's formula of 'God among the dead' is offensive to orthodox
and pure Christocentrics. Moltmann's formula of 'the crucified God' is
offensive to theologians who following Chalcedon talk about God's time-
less being. Anyone who with reference to God's becoming man says with
the First Vatican Council that God revealed Himself, His being, has
usually overlooked the doctrine of grace, has usually overlooked
soteriology. In an ontological Christology, God is too easily reduced to
being equated with Himself. He is equal to Himself even when He reveals
Himself in the death of the man Jesus. If only He remained equal to
Himself, God would be able to predict Himself, to include Himself in His
own reckoning—even when He becomes poor in Jesus. The *semper idem*
of Vatican strategists of revelation deduced from God's equality with
Himself is 'bourgeois'—precisely because it appeals to a God who is
understood ontologically and who remains equal to Himself to the point
of predictability. The temptation to cast an eye over God's accounts, to

keep an eye on God, is not resisted by all strategists of revelation. It took the theology of the cross to show that this is an un-Christian temptation.

5. DOES THE PRACTICE OF TRANSCENDENTAL MEDITATION END IN AN EQUATION?

In revealing Himself God shows who He is. God thus necessarily shows Himself. About this there is no doubt. Nevertheless there is a distinction between God's revelation of Himself and His saving act. From the strictly theological point of view revelation is defined by God: what God reveals is necessarily Himself. God's saving act, however, God's grace, is something that may be looked for by men but is freely bestowed by God. On this Eberhard Jüngel has written: 'That God does what He is able to do, that He has recapitulated Himself in His revelation, is something that does not rest on necessity but is rather grace'.[6]

God, who is holy, can necessarily only show Himself as holy. This too is something that man looks for and expects. But how and when God's holiness becomes salvation for men is something that depends not on human expectation but on God's free initiative alone. The logic in which holiness and salvation can together be the object of thought is not the logic of an equation but of the dialectic. In it two statements are considered together: one of higher value, God's holiness, and one that is significant but of a lower value, God's salvation in the experience of men and women. God is always something more, was what the scholastics were already saying when they were discussing dialectically God's holiness and God's salvation among men. The dialectic of salvation and holiness became a kind of guide for the determination of human existence.

From this dialectic Karl Rahner, Magnus Löhrer and Walter Kasper have made a transcendental guide.[7] They ask and discuss how a human being becomes a Christian and how the Christian always comes closer to God's holiness. God's becoming man, God as salvation for men, is brought into a transcendental relationship with the process of man's humanisation: becoming more human, more Christian, more like God.

This is an anthropological Christology. If it remains historical, then the dialectical tension between God's holiness and God's salvation persists indissolubly. It is only a transcendentality that is interpreted in dialectical terms that escapes the temptation of wanting to become equal to God. In concrete terms this is a postulate for transcendental meditation. If transcendental meditation tries to raise itself up to God's level, then Hegel's temptation is not far distant: the spirit becoming aware of itself becomes absolute spirit. Spirit becomes the Holy Spirit, God's spirit. The experience of salvation turns into the experience of holiness, into the divinisation of the consciousness in which man becomes human.

I am not ·saying that transcendental meditation does not resist this temptation. Indeed, it maintains the eschatological distinction or the analogy between the human and the divine spirit. But this objection is derived from dogmatic theology, from doctrine, not from the practice of transcendental meditation. The whole point of this practice is to assimilate the human consciousness to the divine. If it reached perfection the practice of this meditation would set the two on an equal level and would conclude with an equation, as the 'bourgeois' consciousness likes to do when the 'bourgeois' talk about good fortune.

6. THE THEOLOGY OF LIBERATION: THEOLOGICAL DIALECTIC BASED ON EXPERIENCE

Theologians of liberation such as Gustavo Gutiérrez or Galilea Segundo advocate the revolutionary transformation of transcendentality, but only of a transcendentality that remains aware of the dialectic between God's holy freedom and God's liberating salvation. The underlying momentum of liberation movements liberation theologians see as looking ahead to the free 'God ahead of us'. Whether verified by the Old or the New Testament theology thus means Exodus theology. On the basis of their transcendental commitment Exodus theologians ask where God is, where in history, and their answer is: 'Here'—but always a little bit ahead. Why ahead? Because the poor are not yet free but are dependent; because the rich are not yet free but cling to possessions; because revolutionary consciousness is caught up in the entanglements of violence; and a neutral attitude is caught up in the entanglements of an apathy that tells itself that nothing can be done. The movement of liberation does not want to liberate just anyone but must liberate everyone from false consciousness: the poor, the rich, the guerrilla fighters, those who are politically inactive, a Church that simply adopts an attitude of neutrality. The liberation movement cannot exclude anyone. Freedom is indivisible. But in practice it is patchy and incomplete. This is the lesson of experience in the liberation movement. Hence liberation theologians know on the basis of their practical experience that we all, all of us together, are not holy as God is in His freedom. God is always ahead of us, even and in fact precisely when thanks to God's salvation we are moving along the paths of freedom.

The dialectic, indispensable in the transcendentality of freedom, is not asserted by liberation theologians as if it were something learned out of a book. It is founded on experience. Dialectic here is the concept that results from practice. Gutiérrez, Galilea, Scannone, Siebeneichler[8] are pushing forward with a soteriology that as a movement of freedom never makes theology and Christology superfluous. Their option for holiness and freedom in God and in Christ remains in a dialectical relationship with the consciousness of freedom that has already been realised in practice.

And this is a consciousness of freedom that cannot exclude anyone. In His freedom God is the God of all men and women. Hence it is His intention that all should come to an awareness of their freedom: the entire people, not just a small handful or the *communauté de base* that has already experienced salvation in the practice of a liberating theology. Starting out from the fundamental principle that God is the God of all men and women locates liberation theology in the field of practice, in a world-wide field. If God is the God of everyone, if God's freedom is the norm of Christian liberation, then when it comes down to practical application what is needed is liberation on a world scale. Liberation theologians cannot dismiss the world from the normative claim of the liberation of everyone. Liberation theology must be concerned with liberation on a world scale if it does not want to abandon a theology that asserts that God is the God of all men and women.

There is the obvious objection that dialogue between north and south, economic and educational projects, liberation on a world scale are certainly necessary; but is this not starting on something that can never be brought to completion?

Comblin and Muñoz, and recently Metz too,[9] take this objection up and say that it is right in a limited sense. For to argue on Hegelian lines, the practice of liberation is carried on by subjects, by a number of individuals who contribute ethically, socially, with sadness and lamentation to the advance of history, and go on doing so until at some later stage society itself becomes the subject of history and becomes the vehicle of the individual's consciousness. 'At some later stage,' say Bloch and Garaudy, for example, it will be like this. Comblin, Muñoz, Metz object that if it is to be like this at some later stage then this concept arrives on the scene too late for today. Today already practical demands are being made on a world scale. Anyone who does not see and grasp this now is engaged in alienating consciousness from practice, because he is taking his orientation from an ideal that today is 'not yet' practical. An ideal that at the moment is merely utopian leads to the capitulation of the subject before the historical demands that are being made on a world scale. This would be a 'bourgeois' capitulation. The 'bourgeois' capitulate in the face of tasks and demands that are not subject to calculation.

Metz sees the consequences of utopian ideals in the person called on to act here and now, but reverses the relationship between the individual and society and stands it on its head. In this reversal he is aided by a biblical theology based on the concept of the people of God: 'The history of the religion of the bible is a history of a people becoming responsible for its own destiny and of the individual within that people similarly becoming responsible. The subject [of history] here is not at all the isolated individual . . . [who] has gained assurance in the consequences of his co-existence with others. The experience of relations with other subjects, whether of solidarity or antagonism, of liberation or anxiety, belong from the start to the constitution of the religious subject, and the question as to the relationship of the individual subject to others has the contrived effect of the product of a late stage of abstraction.' In the practical living out of its history God's people has experiences, and it is in the authority of these experiences that the complete process takes place of the people becoming responsible for its own actions and destiny and of the individual in this people similarly becoming subject and not object. In the recollections of the people the 'name of God' denotes the fact 'that the utopian ideal of the liberation of everyone to become subjects in a manner in keeping with human dignity does not remain a pure projection, as indeed it would be and would remain if there were only utopian ideals and no God'.

Fundamental theology believes in God, not in some Utopian idea. This belief in God finds its practical expression in the people's experiences of history—a practical expression in which God's people from the start was always the subject of history and in which today it reminds its individual members of this fact. This is recalled in such a way that the defeatism of the 'bourgeois' subject in his or her consciousness is done away with through these historical accounts of the people's attainment of responsibility and of the authoritative experiences of individuals in the people's history.

It is under the name of God that the Church as the people of God, that Christians within the people of God are summoned to abandon any capitulation before wordly demands. Through the grace of God they are in a position to be the subject of the liberation of everyone and their enjoyment of human dignity. The Church as the people of God does not indulge in 'bourgeois' calculations to see if liberation is possible on a world scale.

At the same time this is a theology of penance that can be given a biblical foundation: in the name of God the people of God is summoned to abandon capitulation in the face of history. In his narrative style Metz includes this theology of penance as critical remembrance.

At the same time this is soteriology in the sense of the new theology of grace of Schillebeeckx, Boff and Ruggieri.[10] In the authority of the experiences of the Church and of the Christians who belong to it belief in salvation becomes a matter of practical application for everyone, the people becomes the subject of history. It is a question of a soteriology that is not a matter of abstract doctrine but is rooted in the authority of experiences of faith. Metz too with his narrative method recalls this with biblical historical accounts.[11] A liberation theology that bases its option on belief in God being the God of all men and women has its eyes on what the people have experienced in the historical process of liberation. This provides a decisive correction to Hegel. In history Hegel concentrates on the individual subject's becoming aware of liberation, and he is followed by transcendental philosophers, Marxist Hegelians, and theologians of transcendental meditation, each in his or her own way.

The correction provided by recent soteriology—'a people becoming responsible for its own destiny and the individual within that people similarly becoming responsible'—has a good biblical basis. Nor is there any doubt about this. The question is simply: does this soteriology replace a Christology? Is it the aim of a liberating theology of salvation to be itself a Christology? Is this possible?

7. SOTERIOLOGY AS PURELY NARRATIVE CHRISTOLOGY?

A few questions must be allowed. What is the origin of liberation theology's knowledge that in the recollections of the people the name of God stands for the realisation that the liberation of all men and women is possible? This is not something it knows simply because this is the way the Bible tells the story. Recourse to biblicism is not something that can be laid to its charge. At least Schillebeeckx, Metz and their pupils are aware and demonstrate that the structure of biblical accounts is 'narrative'— which means that here experiences are recounted that go back to experiences undergone by an entire people 'under the name of God' and are still undergone today by the Church as the people of God. Structurally this cannot be disputed. But it is not yet a sufficient argument. Communities formed on the basis of the Christian story and the people of God as such a community can in fact from the authority of their experiences with God have the consciousness of being not the object but the subject of history. If the people has this consciousness, then in Exodus-theology the talk is of 'discipleship'—following God by following Christ. And this is correct. The attitude that is meant by this is not just a conscious discipleship but one that is lived—conscious discipleship in the practice of discipleship by an entire people.

But what would the situation be if the people were following a false God, one whom it has dreamed up for itself, one that did not exist outside its consciousness? Even in this case the authority of its experiences could still carry conviction. Who for example would deny the radical Christocentrics the authority of their experience? The Russian Christocentrics—Bulgakov and Solovyev—worked consistently on a narrative basis. Of course, in relation to the demands that are made today and not the day after tomorrow on a world scale and in relation to practical application, the theoretical principles of the people that is the subject of history are more convincing than Hegelian ones. But with this convincingness the question is posed in that much more radical a way: 'Are you he who is to come?'

Until the contrary is proved I am of the opinion that the new soteriology, the doctrine of salvation, of grace, of the experience of faith and liberation, is an improvement on all previous efforts. But along with Meyer and Schlochtern[12] I am obliged to say that in the absence of a Christology and theology proceeding by means of rational argument it remains too much a matter of narration. Schillebeeckx, after he had written his soteriology and had made it credible on the basis of narrative assertion, noted: 'Now I had to write a Christology.'

As a critical starting-point for this Christology I would suggest a question which is to be found in soteriology as orthopraxy and which concerns the latter's category 'discipleship'. The question is: Is this category of 'discipleship' which is valid in soteriology also a valid category in Christology? My answer, for which the reasons have yet to be given, is: No, it is not.

8. THE CATEGORY 'DISCIPLESHIP' DOES NOT BELONG TO CHRISTOLOGY

In this new soteriology the option for God's humanity, freedom and holiness comes in its practical application under the category 'discipleship'.

Leonardo Boff's Christological guidelines for Christianity and sacramental man, those by Giuseppe Ruggieri or Ronaldo Muñoz for the *communauté de base*, those by Johannes B. Metz for Christian religious orders, those by Juan Carlos Scannone and Flávio Siebeneichler for popular Catholicism: these and other attempts at providing a soteriological orientation amount to the category of a practical doctrine of grace called discipleship.[13] Discipleship has become a category of soteriology. Keyed as it is from the sociological point of view to large or small groups within the Church, the category of discipleship also becomes a matter of practical application. Both are points in its favour.

If discipleship is a category that has good biblical as well as practical foundations, the question then arises why we should still have a Christology before or alongside soteriology. To this there is to begin with a simple answer: If discipleship is the category for Christians who follow Jesus as his disciples, then it cannot in the same sense be a category for Christ. The statement that Jesus Christ is his own disciple is an unusable tautology.

The second point is that this objection is not just one of merely logical validity. There are material reasons against taking over into Christology from soteriology, where it is valid, the category of discipleship. For example, Giuseppe Ruggieri includes discipleship in the community under the practical category of obedience.[14] Alluding to Phil. 2:5-11 he speaks of Christ's obedience. Later when dealing with the theology of the community he once again addresses himself to obedience, this time with reference to Hans Urs von Balthasar. On this occasion he interprets it as 'deeper insight'. This may be hermeneutically possible. In its practical application it leads to consequences that cannot be justified for men and women. From a hermeneutical point of view Christ's obedience, 'like' the obedience of Christians, was a deeper insight—into God's wisdom and self-giving, as Ruggieri says. In fact the hymn in the letter to the Philippians is a summons to this kind of assimilation to Christ in following Christ in discipleship: 'Strive among yourselves for the deeper insight that was in Christ Jesus' (Phil. 2:5). It is not only with regard to hermeneutics that a similarity exists between Christ's obedience and the obedience of Christians. The similarity is demanded by Paul for the sake of salvation and thus soteriologically. But when it comes to practical application there is a difference.

Christ was obedient unto death, even death on a cross; but one can be a Christian in the service of the brethren without undergoing torture and death on the cross. In his obedience Christ became a martyr in the sense of shedding his blood. But who could justify sending his or her fellow-Christians or an entire community of Christians into the martyrdom of shedding their blood by reference to the category of discipleship labelled obedience? There is a difference between the martyr Christ who voluntarily went to his death; the Christian martyrs who became martyrs under the force of political pressure; and the confessors who are at work in the liberating practical life of the community theoretically aware, and it is to be hoped only theoretically, of the ultimate bloody consequences that their actions might lead them to. Erik Peterson has worked out these distinctions, often sarcastically, often seriously. Precisely because Peterson's conclusion, that politics has died under the cross of Jesus, is idealistic and therefore historically false, there exists in the practical living out of discipleship a distinction between Jesus, who went voluntarily to the death of the cross, the martyrs and us ordinary Christians who die in our beds.

Jesus carrying the cross belongs to Christology and only thereafter to soteriology. Christology and soteriology become 'bourgeois' if they are turned into purely hermeneutical equations that in discipleship put everyone on the same level.

Christ voluntarily carrying the cross belongs to Christology, to theology, and only by derivation to soteriology. It was in the freedom of God that He died on the cross.

Once again, and this applies to Boff and Ruggieri too, my view is that the new soteriology is better than its predecessors. It is for that reason that I subject it to criticism. But—soteriology without Christology?

Soteriology without Christology could in any case have 'discipleship' as a category. But discipleship does not yet provide a rational basis for freedom, even if it makes liberation credible when it comes to practical applications on a world scale. To provide a rational basis for freedom and not just for liberation would be a task for a theological Christology. Admittedly soteriology is not left hanging in the air without this Christology. It has its feet on the ground of experiences. But it can find itself in mid-air without the proposition, suitably established by rational arguments: 'Christ is our freedom.'

Translated by Robert Nowell

Notes

1. R. Muñoz 'The Function of the Poor in the Church' in *Concilium* (April 1977) vol. 10 no. 4.

2. On tendencies in Christology to the left or to the right, see H. Küng *Menschwerdung Gottes* (Freiburg Basle Vienna 1970) p. 611-622.

3. There is more on this in A. Grillmeier 'Die theologische und sprachliche Vorbereitung der christologischen Formal von Chalkedon' in *Chalkedon,* vol. I, esp. p. 199; W. Elert *Der Ausgang der altkitchlichen Christologie* p. 71-132; H. Küng *Existiert Gott?* (Munich 1978) p. 748, 750; H. Küng *20 Thesen zum Christsein* (Munich 1975) p. 11-12, 23 ff. 53 ff.

4. H. U. von Balthasar *Mysterium Paschale: Mysterium Salutis* vol. III fasc. 2, p. 133 326.

5. J. Moltmann *Perspektiven der Theologie* (Munich 1968) p. 47-8; J. Moltmann *Der gekreuzigte Gott* (Munich 1973).

6. E. Jüngel *Gottes Sein ist im Werden* (Tübingen 1967) p. 118; a similar if more functional approach is taken by W. Kasper *Christologie im Präsens.*

7. K. Rahner *Schriften zur Theologie* vol. I p. 169-222; vol. III p. 35-60; vol. V p. 183-221; vol. VII p. 133-136; M. Löhrer *Mysterium Salutis* (Einsiedeln 1965-76) vol. II esp. p. 311; also W. Kasper *Einführung in den Glauben* p. 52, 56; W. Kasper *Jesus der Christus* (Mainz 1974).

8. G. Gutiérrez 'Praxis de liberación y fe cristiana' in *Signos de liberación*; S. Galilea 'Para una Iglesia del Pueblo' in *Ediciones vicaria de la solidaridad, reflexion 7*; J. C. Scannone 'Fe Cristiana y Cambio Social en America Latina' in *Fe y Secularidad* p. 353-372; F. B. Siebeneichler *Catolicismo Popular— Pentecostismo Kirche* (sic) p. 171-199.

9. J. Comblin *Teologia de la Misión*; R. Muñoz *Solidaridad Liberadora— Misión de Iglesia*; J. B. Metz *Glaube in Geschichte und Gesellschaft* p. 45 ff. together with p. 120 ff.

10. E. Schillebeeckx *Glaubensinterpretation* p. 139 ff.; E. Schillebeeckx *Jezus, het verhaal van een levende* (Bloemendaal 1974); E. Schillebeeckx *Christus und die Christen* p. 27, 29, 461 ff., 767; L. Boff *Jésus-Christ Libérateur* p. 247 ff.; G. Ruggieri *Christliche Gemeinde und 'Politische Theologie'* p. 90 ff.

11. J. B. Metz *op. cit.* p. 3 ff. together with p. 77 ff., p. 136 ff. together with p. 161 ff.

12. J. Meyer zu Schlochtern *Glaube—Sprache—Erfahrung: Zur Begründungsfähigkeit der religiösen Überzeugung.*

13. Besides the works cited in note 8 above, see J. B. Metz *Zeit der Orden? Zur Mystik und Politik der Nachfolge* (Freiburg 1977).

14. G. Ruggieri *op. cit.* p. 57 ff. together with p. 103-4, p. 130 ff.; E. Peterson *Marginalien zur Theologie* p. 17 ff., 27; E. Peterson *Theologische Traktate* p. 165-224.

Arend van Leeuwen, Bert van Dijk and Theo
Salemink

Crisis and Criticism of
'Bourgeois' (*Burgerlijke*) Theology

IN A theological text, as in any ideological production, an intervention is
made in a field in which the positions have all been occupied for a long
time. At the centre of that field, there is a dominant theological paradigm.
At the same time, however, a number of attempts to break out of this
paradigm will already have been made.

The dominant paradigm in theology was formed long ago during the
periods of Roman imperialism and medieval feudalism. It is characterised
by a twofold structure of nature and supernature, secular and salvation
history, politics and faith and liberation and redemption. This structure
appears with particular clarity in the familiar form of a natural theology in
which there is an intrinsic bond between nature and supernature. In that
theology, these two elements are seen within the perspective of each
other. They also support and strengthen each other.

This paradigm could no longer be unquestioningly accepted in the new
'bourgeois' society with its completely different class relationships. To
begin with, the theology of the Reformation was able to continue to
function within the new relationships of capitalist society based on trade.
New and lasting tensions were, however, caused by the emergence of the
new form of capitalism based on industry in the eighteenth and
nineteenth centuries. The rising 'bourgeoisie' with its great self-assurance
was unable to accept either the traditional scholastic theology or the later
reformed theology, both of which emphasised the dualism between
nature and supernature. Theology was therefore forced into a confrontation with the 'bourgeois' consciousness and threatened with the
loss of its right to exist in industrial society. An attempt was made in

Reformed Christianity, which had already been involved in confrontation with 'bourgeois' attitudes, to bring theology up to date. The result was the so-called liberal theology, in which the achievements of 'bourgeois' scientific knowledge and the ideals of the new 'bourgeois' philosophy were incorporated, but the structure of the earlier theological paradigm was not completely rejected. The Protestant liberal theology of the nineteenth century, then, was fundamentally an embellishment of the 'bourgeois' consciousness.

After 1870, the revolutionary phase passed and the 'bourgeois' had to defend itself with all the means at its disposal against an internal crisis and the external threat of socialism, which was increasing in strength. One result of this situation was the production in the Catholic Church of a popular form of theology adapted to the 'bourgeois' consciousness. This was neo-scholasticism, which Ernst Bloch described as a modern ideology of the class conflict imposed from above.

The twentieth century has been characterised by an imperialistic form of capitalism and a radical state of economic and political crisis. It has become clear, in this situation, that the results produced in the two earlier confrontations between Christianity and the 'bourgeois' consciousness that we have outlined above were not sufficient to deal with the theological problems of the present century. What was needed was a further confrontation in which the status of theology and in particular of the theological paradigm would itself be seriously called into question. In this article, then, we have chosen to outline this confrontation on the basis of the work of three representative theologians—Hans Küng and his theology of the *aggiornamento*, Karl Barth and his dialectical theology and Arend van Leeuwen and his economic theology.

This most recent confrontation, or rather, series of confrontations, as represented by the three authors whose work is discussed in this article, has been marked by a number of aims. In the first place, the theologians in question have been concerned to bring theology up to date, in other words, to make it function properly at the level of developed 'bourgeois' society. In the second place, an attempt has been made to resolve the struggle between giving theology a 'bourgeois' status and depriving it of that status. Finally, in the third place, the status of theology itself has been radically called into question.

1. HANS KÜNG: THEOLOGY IN DIALOGUE WITH THE 'BOURGEOIS' PHILOSOPHER HEGEL

More than twenty years ago, the Catholic theologian Hans Küng became widely known because of his thesis on the doctrine of justification in the work of Karl Barth, in which he dealt, in so far as it was possible for a Catholic theologian to do this, with the most progressive position in the theology of the Reformed Church. Since that time, Küng has become even more widely known as a critical theologian within the Catholic Church. His great work on Hegel, which was published on the two hundreth anniversary of the birth of the German philosopher,[1] is far less well known. Küng himself regards it as his most important work and rightly, because its fundamental theme is that of the crisis of theology in a 'bourgeois' society.

The central question in this book is that of God himself. Küng points out that the traditional theological attitudes towards God[2] and Jesus Christ[3] are no longer tenable in contemporary 'bourgeois' society, in which the predominant view is that man's nature and that of God are radically different, with the result that the God-man can no longer be accepted.[4] He also points out, however, that this traditional theological paradigm—to use our term—could not even provide a solution to the problems of the period in which it was first developed and this is because it really hardly touched the centre of the original New Testament message of Jesus Christ. The classical Christology, which is at the heart of this paradigm, was formulated on the basis of the Greek metaphysical idea of God. This metaphysical concept of the absolutely unchangeable God is, either directly or indirectly, at the basis of the Church's traditional teaching.[5]

In an attempt to solve this dilemma between the metaphysical view and the biblical concept of God, Küng looks to Hegel.[6] In Küng's opinion, the central message of Hegel's teaching is to be found in his dialectical identification of God and man in the 'absolute spirit'.[7] The problem that arises here is that, in Hegel's view, the traditional antitheses between spirit and matter (Bloch),[8] the twofold structure of nature and super-nature (van Dijk and Salemink) and the contrast between God and man (Küng)[9] are cancelled out at the level of this absolute spirit. Küng does not, however, accept this and insists that there is neither a separation between nor an intermingling of divine and human nature and that there is therefore no radical abolition of the fundamental structure of the traditional paradigm.

Küng is anxious to correct what he calls the 'constructed schematism'[10] and the 'monism of the spirit'[11] in which the distinction between nature and supernature is cancelled out in Hegel's teaching and therefore looks to David Friedrich Strauss and Søren Kierkegaard. He refuses to give up Hegel's emphasis on the historicity of God, Strauss' on the historicity of Jesus and Kierkegaard's on man's existential encounter with the New Testament message of Christ and the essential function of faith.[12]

Küng's study, then, is fundamentally a confrontation between Christian theology and Hegel's 'bourgeois' philosophy. Küng is extremely conscious of Hegel's own complex form of Christianity.[13] At one level of interpretation, Küng points out, Hegel's philosophy can be seen as an attempt to make Christianity acceptable to modern man, but, at another level, it can also be interpreted as an attempt to deny the value of religious understanding. Kierkegaard was also aware of this ambiguity in Hegel's teaching and he therefore rejected the idea of trying to prove the existence of God—and Christ—by means of philosophy. Küng points out that Kierkegaard was not concerned to bring about the absolute paradox speculatively, since that paradox was, in his opinion, only accessible to faith.[14] In opposition to Hegel, Küng returns here to the traditional theological position that Christianity is, at the existential level at least, an individual decision that cannot be justified by reason alone.

We may therefore conclude that, in his attempt to re-interpret the traditional Christian concept of God at the level of the 'bourgeois' consciousness of today,[15] Küng comes down firmly in favour of preserving the classical twofold structure of reality and the balance between heaven and earth. In his attempt to redefine Christology for modern man too, he re-affirms the Chalcedonian statement (A.D. 451) that there are in Christ 'two natures, without confusion, without change, without division and without separation'.[16] Küng certainly does not make a naïve connection between nature and supernature, but he upholds the classical theological paradigm. This, of course, tends to make him all the more naïve with regard to the 'bourgeois' consciousness.

2. KARL BARTH: TOWARDS A CRITICISM OF 'BOURGEOIS' THEOLOGY

As we have seen, Küng has tried in his book on Hegel's theological thought to make the Christian tradition intelligible to members of contemporary 'bourgeois' society. The Protestant theologian Karl Barth followed a different course of action, but with a similar aim in view. He recognised that 'bourgeois' philosophy could not be used as a hermeneutical instrument without serious difficulties. He knew that the 'bourgeois' consciousness was not neutral and that it was firmly tied to the interests of one class in society. In his two-volume work on Protestant theology in the nineteenth century,[17] he showed clearly that the prevailing theology in the reformed churches during that and the preceding century was ultimately no more than an extension of the complex self-consciousness of the new 'bourgeoisie'.

Catholic theology since the First Vatican Council and up to the Second Vatican Council had a medieval appearance, but it was in fact no more than a variant of the same 'bourgeois' ideology. It contained all the totalitarian aspects of the 'bourgeois' consciousness that was no longer revolutionary in spirit since 1870, but was fighting to remain alive. Barth called the struggle between liberalism and the Catholic social teaching of the period a 'family quarrel'.[18]

On the basis of his criticism of both the Protestant and the Catholic forms of 'bourgeois' theology, Barth tried to formulate a new dialectical theology which neither relied on earlier structures nor exposed itself to the ideology of the 'bourgeoisie'. It is possible to say that Barth's *Church Dogmatics* constitute the most consistent criticism of religion that has appeared in this century. He mercilessly condemned the prevailing form of Christianity as the 'opium of the people' and the ideology of the ruling class. He defined religion as man's attempt to justify and sanctify himself in the presence of a self-willed and arbitrary image of God that he has fashioned for himself.[19] He contrasted this version of religion with God's revelation of himself as the discontinuation of religion. For him, God was completely different, the one who put an end to man's sanctification of himself and who was the total antithesis to the 'bourgeois' consciousness. Man's natural knowledge could never be the source of his knowledge of the God who was completely different. Scripture, which continues to exist as a foreign body in our society, is the only source of our knowledge of God.

This, then, is a brief summary of the way in which Barth tried to escape from the influence of the prevailing 'bourgeois' theology. It was, of course, an escape upwards, an exodus from history in an attempt to save history from the totalitarian self-deification of the prevailing powers in society. The dramatic tension and the commitment to human history involved in this great undertaking become clear when we remember that Barth and his Dutch follower, K. H. Miskotte,[20] were working during the critical period of the nineteen-thirties, when fascism was rapidly gaining ground throughout Europe. Biblical theology, in which the complete difference of God is stressed, and the socialist tradition would therefore seem to be almost the only effective ideological instruments that can be used against such totalitarian systems as fascism.

3. AREND VAN LEEUWEN: AN OUTLINE OF AN ECONOMIC THEOLOGY

Arend van Leeuwen, who teaches in the Faculty of Theology at the Catholic University of Nijmegen, specialising in the theology of social action, works within the tradition of Karl Barth, whose theology he came to know during the period of European crisis and the Second World War. After the war, he was active in the mission in Indonesia, where he came into contact with the questions that were being asked by a Third World society in a state of revolution. This experience led to the development of his own form of a theology of secularisation in his book *Christianity in World History* (1964).[21] This was followed a few years later by *Develop-*

ment through Revolution (1968),[22] which should properly be called a political theology. Since 1968, van Leeuwen has been more systematically concerned with a debate with the Marxist analysis of society and this resulted in his two-volume work, *Critique of Heaven and Earth* (1972).[23] The text of his Gifford lectures at Aberdeen University is included in this work, in which he is indebted, among others, to Barth.

Van Leeuwen has taken part in a very special way in the debate about the 'bourgeois' nature of theology. It is obvious from all that he has written that he respects Barth greatly as a theologian who has tried to make a radical criticism of 'bourgeois' society really effective in the sphere of theology, but it is equally clear that he believes that Barth did not go far enough. Where he failed was in not incorporating Marx's criticism of the 'bourgeois' ideology, as outlined in *Das Kapital* and *Theorien über den Mehrwert*, into his own criticism of 'bourgeois' theology.

Van Leeuwen has certainly tried to do that. In his *Critique of Heaven and Earth*, he points to the change that took place in Marx's development. The younger Marx was concerned with the criticism of religion and completed the work in this sphere that had been initiated by Feuerbach. His later experience in the sphere of politics, however, led him to criticise law and politics and ultimately political economy. Marx's practical experience and theoretical understanding both led him to recognise that the 'bourgeois' consciousness was not governed either by religion or by law and politics, but by economics. An ideology based on economics, he concluded, had taken the place of the religious or political ideologies of earlier societies. Economics, then, formed the 'everyday religion' of 'bourgeois' society or, as van Leeuwen has said on several occasions, the scribes of the Law in capitalist society are the professors of economics.

As we pointed out above, van Leeuwen thinks that Barth did not go far enough in his attempt to break away from 'bourgeois' theology. This, van Leeuwen has suggested, is because, although he was very consistent in his criticism of religion, he did not criticise either the legal and political aspects of 'bourgeois' society or the political economy on which the 'bourgeois' consciousness is ultimately based. Because of this, Barth's theology does not penetrate to the heart of 'bourgeois' society and is therefore not quite up to date.

Going even further in his assessment of Barth's dialectical theology, van Leeuwen also believes that the Swiss theologian went in the wrong direction. His appeal to Scripture as the revelation of God, the completely different one, placed him in a position that was diametrically opposed to the prevailing 'bourgeois' consciousness, but at the same time outside history. Van Leeuwen describes Barth's theology as 'a leap from total darkness into total light, a *creatio ex nihilo*, but a leap in which history is "superseded". It is a tremendous merit of Barth's *Dogmatics* that in them the doctrine of God's revelation is developed out of the history of the Incarnation of the Word and the doctrine of the Trinity derives from that. Yet this gain becomes a loss, because no real relation is established with our history. The dialectic, it would seem, is not able to overcome the dualism'.[24]

In developing his own economic theology, on the other hand, van Leeuwen has always taken care to remain firmly within the framework of human history and has moreover taken Marx's materialistic conception of history as his point of departure. History, then, for van Leeuwen, has developed in a dialectical process of conflict in which certain irreversible transformations have taken place in which both completely new historical situations have been brought about and a distance has been created in history from other historical periods and different forms of society.

One of these historical transformations is, according to van Leeuwen, the disappearance of religion, law and politics from the centre of 'bourgeois' ideology and their replacement by economics. In the forms of society in Asia Minor and the Roman Empire, in which the Jewish and Christian traditions developed, religion and politics were the dominant influences. It is therefore not possible simply to interpret the criticism of the prevailing religion and of the state that is contained in the Bible and apply this to contemporary 'bourgeois' society, as modern hermeneutics would seem to suggest. There is, in other words, not only a difference in language, culture and historical development between Judaeo-Christian society and contemporary 'bourgeois' society—there is also a fundamental difference in the two social and ideological structures. Only an exact knowledge of the new form of society and its special ideological structure can, in van Leeuwen's opinion, create the conditions under which theology can operate properly. On the other hand, this knowledge may show that theology and the biblical tradition are out of date. Van Leeuwen has therefore come to the conclusion that the only possible course of action is to go through the eye of the Marxist needle. To do this, theology itself must also be transformed. It can, in other words, no longer function as a theology of secularisation or as a political theology.

4. PROBLEMS AND QUESTIONS[25]

In this third series of confrontations between theology and the 'bourgeois' consciousness, an increasing intensity and a progressively more radical criticism can be detected in the work of Hans Küng, Karl Barth and Arend van Leeuwen in that order.

Küng has not really resolved the increasing discrepancy between theology and the 'bourgeois' consciousness. What he has in fact done is to set theology free from a number of naïve ideas that had given scandal to the 'bourgeois' consciousness. In doing this, he has done no more than the liberal theologians of the eighteenth and nineteenth centuries. His most important achievement is that he has done this for the Catholic tradition.

Barth knew that the traditional theology had come to an end in 'bourgeois' society and that there was a great need for a new theological method. He believed that he had satisfied this need in providing his dialectical theology. He also thought that theology should not, because of the subversive scriptural tradition, be exposed unconditionally to the consciousness of the ruling class, by which, of course, he meant the 'bourgeoisie'. He therefore believed that it was not sufficient to develop any new theology. It had to be a partial theology, in other words, a non-'bourgeois' theology.

Following Barth, van Leeuwen thinks, however, that his master did not, as we have seen, go far enough in his confrontation with 'bourgeois' society and that he left human history prematurely, as it were, and entered the sphere of salvation history because he did not take Marx's very radical criticism of 'bourgeois' society into consideration in his own criticism. In this unjustified way, then, the traditional theological paradigm was spared from being placed in a radically critical situation.

Van Leeuwen's confrontation with 'bourgeois' society and its ideology is certainly the most far-reaching in that he has included Marx's criticism in this confrontation. In this context, two questions of some importance arise. The first is: To what extent is van Leeuwen's confrontation really radical, in other words, does he too spare the traditional theological paradigm from crisis and collapse? A second and related question is: Is van Leeuwen's theology really non-'bourgeois', in other words, is it partial and on the side of socialism? We will attempt, in the second part of this article, to resolve this difficulty and overcome this suspicion by asking van Leeuwen himself three critical questions which aim to test the solidity rather than the validity of his confrontation.

Question 1

Van Leeuwen says that Marx was a theologian to the extent that he interpreted 'bourgeois' society, within the context of history, as the 'pre-history of human society'.[26] He also spoke of a 'human materialism'.[27] In view of the importance of the recent debate in Marxist circles between those, such as Louis Althusser, who uphold the theoretical anti-humanism of the later Marx and those who insist, as Lucien Sève does, on the philosophical humanism of the younger Marx, we are bound to ask whether van Leeuwen has not been tempted by his own theological background to regard Marx as a theologian and a humanist and therefore,

for apologetic reasons, to transform Marx's analysis into an introduction
to theology.

Question 2

Marx concluded his *Kapital* with a section on 'The Classes', but this
section is only two pages long and incomplete. Marx originally intended
to publish a further four volumes after the volume on capital, in which he
proposed to deal with political theory. This presents us with a problem in
any consideration of Marx's ideas and also in any assessment of van
Leeuwen's work. Van Leeuwen has certainly taken over Marx's
economic theory and has used it fruitfully to transform theology. He has,
however, hardly considered Marx's political theory at all. We are therefore bound to ask what relationship exists between the critical economic
theology of van Leeuwen and the organisation of various classes in
society and especially the socialist movement.

Question 3

Questions inevitably arise not only because of van Leeuwen's involvement with Marxist theory, but also because of his view of the function of
the Christian tradition and the part played in it by theology. On the one
hand, he clearly regards the prevailing form of Christianity and its theology as a special form of 'bourgeois' ideology and therefore as a legitimate
object of criticism. On the other hand, however, he has always insisted
that there are certain elements in the Christian tradition that provide a
point of departure for this criticism, with the result that, subject to certain
conditions, the Christian tradition is also a legitimate subject of criticism.
What, then, is their relationship with each other?

Has van Leeuwen, then, not perhaps made rather facile use of Marx's
theory in order to achieve for theology the miracle that theology has not
for several centuries been able to achieve for itself? This miracle is the
bringing up to date of theology and its liberation from its 'bourgeois'
stranglehold.

5. AREND VAN LEEUWEN'S REACTION

To Question 1

With regard to the first question about Marx as a theologian and a
humanist, I should like to point out that I would not want to use the term
'humanist' as an ethical category in order to make Marx more accessible
to theology. I entirely reject this interpretation of Marx's teaching, which
has unfortunately tended to dominate the whole of the recent dialogue
between Christians and Marxists. I use the term 'humanist' rather as an
objective category and in this I am simply following Marx's own terminology.

Marx characterised the history of mankind in its successive economic phases, culminating in the present period of 'bourgeois' relationships based on production and consumption, as the 'pre-history of human society'. This surely points very clearly to the future birth of 'human society conceived in the womb of "bourgeois" society'. This is Marx's own definition at the beginning of *Das Kapital*. On the same page we find such statements as the 'consciousness of men' being determined by their social condition and 'mankind always sets itself only such tasks as it can solve'.[28] These statements were, it should be noted, made by the older Marx.

Anything that we may say, however, about whether or not Marx was a humanist does not really go to the heart of the matter, since this first question expresses a suspicion about the correctness of my assessment of Marx as a theologian. I am, in other words, suspected of trying to make Marx, the radical humanist, into a disguised theologian.

My counter-question is this: Is the division between anthropology and theology as absolute as has been suggested? Surely theology is conducted at the same level as any form of anthropology? I would also add that the opposite is also true, in other words, that we cannot undertake anthropological experiments in a laboratory from which theology is totally excluded. We cannot do this for the same reason that it is impossible to study theology divorced from the study of man. In other words, on this earth, where all men exist and think collectively, theology forms part of our atmosphere and is something that we breathe in and out. What is more, we only have to dig in the ground to unearth theological finds at the most unexpected moments. They are there in the earth beneath our feet.

Let me give one example of what I mean. Anyone reading *Das Kapital* from cover to cover will be able to follow a scarlet thread through the book. This thread is 'fetishism'. It surely speaks volumes that Marx, who was himself a product of the Enlightenment, should have turned to theology or the science of comparative religion for a term, denoting a form of idolatry, in his attempt to sum up his critical analysis of 'bourgeois' society in a single, terse definition.

It would seem, then, that it is precisely during the historical period in which the 'bourgeois' citizen, who has come of age and is fully enlightened and conscious of himself, deceives himself into thinking that he has at last left theology behind and is henceforth only concerned with the study of man that the anthropological mask is stripped away to reveal the theological face beneath.

I would therefore like to ask a rather challenging counter-question: How is it possible to manage without theology in any study of modern history, that is, a study of society in the eighteenth and nineteenth centuries, the period of the Enlightenment and the Counter-

Enlightenment? If we think of the subject under discussion here alone, we cannot deny that the history of socialism and Marxism has been full of theological debate. Ernst Bloch's rediscovery of Utopia would not have given rise to a theology of hope if the socialist Utopia had not been exposed as a foundling by theology. The relationship between Marx and Hegel would, moreover, not have overshadowed the debate within Marxist circles up to the present day if it had proved possible to break the link binding Marx's thought to Hegel's trinitarian philosophy of history.

To Question 2

The second question is more concerned with politics. Behind this comment that I have taken Marx's economic theory into account in my theology, but have failed to consider his political theory systematically I detect a question about the relationship within Marx's thought and the Marxist tradition as a whole between economic theory and political theory.

In answer to this question, I would say that there is no political theory in the real sense of the word in Marx's major work. This void has been filled in many different ways by various Marxist theories that have been evolved since Marx himself was writing, but, so far at least, Marxists have not produced any political theory that can be regarded as equal in depth, radical analysis and critical consistency to Marx's own criticism of the political economy of 'bourgeois' society. Generally speaking, there have been three main tendencies in political theory since Marx. These are Eduard Bernstein's social democratic revisionism in Western Europe, Stalin's form of socialism in one country and Trotsky's idea of the world revolution of the proletariat.

The theories underlying these three great political movements can be summed up in the following broad definitions. Revisionism was, in a word, ultimately based on Kant's critical rationalism. Stalin's theory—and praxis—of socialism in one country was developed in accordance with Hegel's theory of law, the second line in his philosophy of history, which was given concrete expression in the German state. Stalin transferred this to Russia. Trotsky followed the first Hegelian line of development, which was concerned with world history.

This was also the line that Marx himself followed in his major work, *Das Kapital*, which was originally entitled 'A Criticism of Political Economy'. In his historical analysis, 'bourgeois' society was the final phase in the 'pre-history of human society' and he was himself particularly concerned with this 'bourgeois' society that was in the process of expanding to become a system embracing the whole world. Indeed, he was so preoccupied with it that he hardly gave any attention to any other system.

I am convinced that we are still fundamentally in the same situation and that 'bourgeois' society is still universally powerful. This universal power is manifested not only in the fact the world market is dominated by multinational enterprises, but also in the existence of the opposing communist bloc. The ideology of this opposing power is shadowy, in that it cannot exist on its own. On the one hand, it is hurrying frantically to catch up with 'bourgeois' society and even to overtake it, while, on the other, it believes that it is compelled to suppress internal signs of an emerging 'bourgeois' ideology. It has, moreover, also reached an impasse by developing a pattern of socialist structures in one country that are in competition with each other, a pattern that corresponds almost exactly to the traditional nationalism of the 'bourgeois' societies. Established socialism has, in other words, in praxis reached an impasse while following the second of Hegel's philosophical lines and this has resulted in the glorification of the state.

I need say no more about Western social democratic revisionism than that it is basically a left-wing variant within 'bourgeois' society, but would like to comment a little less briefly on the first line of Hegel's philosophy which was followed by Marx. This was directly concerned with world history and the whole of mankind. It has never in fact been given a concrete political form anywhere in the world, but it has continued to make itself felt in a persistent criticism, on the one hand, within the debate in western and in third world countries between Marxists and others and, on the other, by left deviationism in the countries of the eastern bloc and probably also in China. No new forms of society at all have been produced in the world in the present century, which is in fact characterised by a progressive intensification of the death pangs of 'bourgeois' society.

Asked about the relationship between my economic theology and Marxist political theory and praxis, then, I would reply with a counter-question: Which theory and which praxis? I am not trying to avoid the challenge that is offered to me in replying in this way. On the contrary, it is a very sober and practical reply. My economic theology is situated firmly within the context of a theoretical and scientific study of Marx's *Kapital* and I am a 'bourgeois' Protestant theologian teaching at a Catholic University. I am also a member of the Dutch social democratic party (Partij van de arbeid). This is a 'revisionist' party which, in my opinion, is the only one which still provides the only real possibility of giving political form in the capitalist society of the Netherlands to the inescapable process of emancipation from the universal power of capital.

To Question 3

This question is concerned with the relationship between three factors—theology, faith and the biblical tradition. The problem here is that my critical theology would seem to be trying to saw off the branch of the tree on which it is sitting. In its present-day 'bourgeois' form in which it functions as the cult of abstract man, Christianity is the object of critical analysis and at the same time it is also the driving force that sets theological criticism in motion. In other words, we are confronted here with the miracle of the *perpetuum mobile* or with the fate of the man who sets fire to himself and in both cases with a *reductio ad absurdum*.

The reference in the critical questions to a tradition within Christianity was correct, because this in principle pointed to the way out of this apparently vicious circle. 'Tradition' is in fact the important category in this dilemma. I believe that it has the following aspects:

(*a*) It represents the broad stream of western Christian history, which is clearly distinguished from the history of India, China, the Islamic world and eastern Christianity.

(*b*) In this western Christian tradition, there is also an active, dynamic and even explosive rhythm of critical rebellion, which has been described by Eugen Rosenstock-Huessy in his *Europäische Revolutionen* as the chain of revolutions which began with the eleventh-century papal revolution and ended with the Russian revolution of 1917.

(*c*) The word 'tradition' is ambiguous. Its first meaning is 'handing on' from hand to hand or from generation to generation. Its second meaning is 'betrayal'. Jesus was 'handed over' to sinners, given up by His own people who betrayed their own Messiah to the pagans. It was in this way and in no other that He became the Messiah of all people. It is also in this way and in no other that He has been handed on in Word and Sacrament from hand to hand and from generation to generation. Wherever that takes place, Jesus' *ekklesia* is present as the Messianic community consisting of Jews and pagans. It is there that 'tradition' is found, that He is handed on and that He is at the same time again and again betrayed, because He is handed over to sinners. As Pascal has pointed out: 'Jesus will be in agony until the end of the world. We must not sleep at that time.'

(*d*) In our western tradition, Scripture, by which I mean the scriptural testimony of God's history with His people from Genesis to Revelation or from the creation to the eschaton, functions within an environment that is determined by three major components. The first is the Church—see (*a*) above—which exists in the explosive rhythm of a revolutionary history—see (*b*) above—which it produces and impels forward on the one hand and of which it is also, on the other hand, the victim, but which it—unlike other cultural and religious institutions—cannot subjugate or control—see (*c*) above. In this constantly changing environment, fresh, cleansing and renewing spring water is always flowing into the stream of progress from the source of Scripture.

(e) Tradition is basically a radical break between the new and the old covenants or the New and the Old Testaments. The fulfilment of the Law was at the same time the end of the Law. A new creation began in Christ. This fundamental dialectical tension has always been present in our western Christian history. Again and again, the established Church has tried to suppress it, but has always failed and its exorcisms and attempts to stamp out heresies have had a boomerang effect. What is officially called the 'Reformation' was really a successful explosion, unlike so many other revolutions which, at least apparently, could be averted.

The whole of modern history is in fact a series of explosions. Feudal Christian society was blown up in the French Revolution and the Communist Manifesto was a time bomb placed under the 'bourgeois' society that had been proclaimed by the French Revolution. This, of course, means that our western Christian history is a completely broken history. Scripture is mediated to us by a broken tradition and Christian faith reflects the testimony of the Bible in a broken mirror. Even this biblical testimony itself is a broken tradition of exodus, exile, diaspora and the Messiah outside the walls, accessible to Israel only via the pagans and to the pagans only via Israel. This means in the twentieth century that it is fundamentally impossible to believe in a direct or naïve way. We are all of us structurally atheists and faith exists in this century in a broken state.

(f) I said at the beginning of my reply to this third question that three factors were involved in this relationship. I will now deal briefly with the third of these factors—theology as a science. I place the emphasis here firmly on the word 'science'. In his study of the structure of the scientific revolutions, the American historian of science, Thomas Kuhn, has shown that our western scientific tradition has never been a continuous process of evolution. It has, on the contrary, always been a chain of fundamental revolutions. As a science, theology has always been involved in this contradictory and self-critical rhythm that has marked the history of science, just as the scientific tradition has also taken part in the history of theology. No modern scientist is, as a scientist, a believing or religious man in the naïve and unquestioning way that Kepler, Newton or Boyle were able to be believers and at the same time scientists three or four hundred years ago. Science has become fundamentally agnostic, even atheistic.

After this rapid tour around the various aspects of tradition, we return to the point from which we set off—the relationship between theology, faith and the biblical tradition. The *perpetuum mobile* is seen to be not miraculous and the negation of self is seen to be not a question of blind fate. My critical theology is in fact sawing off the branch on which it is sitting, but, in this apparently suicidal activity, it is taking part in a dialectical rhythm that is at the heart of the mystery of our western Christian history.

6. CONCLUSION

This article has taken the form of a debate in which a variety of positions have been outlined. It also indicates the dilemma of the 'crisis and criticism of "bourgeois" theology'. The fundamental questions that have been raised in the preceding sections cannot be answered in full within the framework of this debate. What may have been brought to light are those ways which can no longer be followed because they seem to have come to a dead end.

At least three ways have to be included within this category. Firstly, there is the theology in which the crisis of the traditional 'bourgeois' theology is considered within the framework of a dialogue with the leading philosopher of the 'bourgeois' consciousness, Hegel, but in which theology itself is not radically called into question. This way is represented in our article by the work of the Catholic theologian Hans Küng.

Secondly, there is the theology in which the crisis of 'bourgeois' theology is discussed only as a theological crisis that can in principle be overcome by a theologian criticism, on condition that a new method is followed. The theologian whom we have chosen in this article to represent this way is Karl Barth.

Thirdly, there is the impasse of the dialogue between Christianity and Marxism, in which humanism is used as a mediating category.

It is only when theologians really understand Marx's radical diagnosis of the crisis of 'bourgeois' society and incorporate these findings into their theological work as a 'crisis and criticism of "bourgeois" theology' that they will be able to break through the magic circle of 'bourgeois' consciousness and bring their work sufficiently up to date to overcome the 'bourgeois' nature of theology. Whether or not this outline of an economic theology will be capable of carrying out this task remains to be seen. It depends mainly on the further development of the transformation of theology itself. Two factors that are necessary here are healthy suspicion and mutual respect.

Translated by David Smith

Notes

1. H. Küng *Menschwerdung Gottes. Eine Einführung in Hegels theologisches Denken als Prolegomena zu einer künftigen Christologie* (Freiburg, Basle and Vienna 1970).

2. H. Küng *op. cit.* p. 558.

3. H. Küng *op. cit.* p. 565-566.

4. H. Küng *op. cit.* p. 33.

5. H. Küng *op. cit.* p. 542, 533, 535-539.

6. H. Küng *op. cit.* p. 556.

7. H. Küng *op. cit.* p. 523, 537.

8. E. Bloch *Das Materialismusproblem, seine Geschichte und Substanz* (Frankfurt 1972) p. 223.

9. H. Küng *op. cit.* p. 553.

10. H. Küng *op. cit.* p. 574.

11. H. Küng *op. cit.* p. 533, 555, 557.

12. H. Küng *op. cit.* p. 578.

13. H. Küng *op. cit.* p. 503-522.

14. H. Küng *op. cit.* p. 577.

15. H. Küng *op. cit.* p. 609.

16. H. Küng *op. cit.* p. 539, 619.

17. K. Barth *Die protestantische Theologie im 19. Jahrhundert. Ihre Vorgeschichte und ihre Geschichte* I and II (Hamburg ³1960).

18. K Barth *Die kirchliche Dogmatik* (Zollikon and Zürich 1960), I, 2, p. 606-637. ET: *Church Dogmatics* (Edinburgh 1960).

19. K. Barth *op. cit.* I, 2, para. 17.

20. K. H. Miskotte *Edda en Thora* (1934); *Wenn die Götter schweigen* (Munich 1963).

21. A. T. van Leeuwen *Christianity in World History. The Meeting of the Faiths of East and West* (Edinburgh 1964).

22. A. T. van Leeuwen *Development through Revolution* (New York 1970).

23. A. T. van Leeuwen *Critique of Heaven and Earth* I and II (New York and London 1972 and 1974).

24. A. T. van Leeuwen *Critique of Heaven and Earth, op. cit.* p. 277.

25. A word of explanation is required here with regard to the unusual form of this section and the next (that is, Sections IV and V). This section has been written by two of the authors of this article, Bert van Dijk and Theo Salemink, who have briefly outlined the problems and formulated the three critical questions that are put to Arend van Leeuwen. The latter has attempted to answer these three questions in the extended following section (V), which is therefore exclusively his contribution. The reader is therefore invited, because of this form, to take part in a debate conducted by the group of three authors, who are responsible for the article as a whole.

26. A. T. van Leeuwen *Critique of Heaven and Earth, op. cit.* p. 282.

27. A. T. van Leeuwen *Critique, op. cit.* p. 292.

28. Marx's complete works *Werke* Vol. 13, p. 9 (Berlin 1964); (Marx Engels *Selected Works* (Moscow 1962) p. 363.

Contributors

GREGORY BAUM was born in Berlin in 1923 but has lived in Canada since 1940 and was ordained to the priesthood in 1954. He is Professor of Theology and Sociology in St Michael's College, Toronto. He is editor of *The Ecumenist* and co-editor of the *Journal of Ecumenical Studies*. His publications include *Man Becoming* (1970), *New Horizon* (1972) and *Religion and Alienation* (1975).

FERNANDO CASTILLO was born in Santiago, Chile, in 1943 and studied theology and sociology at the universities of Santiago, Münster and Sussex. He has taught both subjects in the Catholic University of Chile. He took his doctorate in theology in 1976, and has published *Theologie aus der Praxis des Volkes* (Munich-Mainz, 1978), and several articles on the ideology and theology of liberation. He is now lecturing at the University of Bielefeld.

BERT VAN DIJK was born in 1946 and worked for a time in an iron foundry in Hengelo. He was educated at a social academy in Sittard and studied theology at Amsterdam, Heerlen and Nijmegen. Since then he has worked as a youth leader in Limburg and, from 1975 onwards, in Twente.

IRING FETSCHER was born in 1922 in Marbach on the Neckar and grew up in Dresden. He has studied philosophy, history and Romance literature. In 1963 he was appointed to the chair of political science at the University of Frankfurt am Main. He has held foreign appointments in Constance, Nijmegen and Vienna, and visiting professorships in New York, Cambridge (Mass.), Canberra and Nijmegen. His other main publications are *Karl Marx and Marxism* (1971); *Modelle der Friedenssicherung* (1972); *Herrschaft und Emanzipation: zur politischen Philosophie des Bürgertums* (Munich 1975); *Terrorismus und Reaktion* (Cologne 1977, 1978).

FRANCIS SCHÜSSLER FIORENZA is Associate Professor, Villanova University. His doctoral thesis at the University of Münster, West Germany, *Eschatology and Progress,* was a study of Ernst Bloch's philosophy of history. He has published articles in various theological and philosophical journals.

AREND VAN LEEUWEN was born in 1918, studied theology at Leiden University and graduated in 1947, with a dissertation on Ghazali as the apologist of Islam. He was chaplain to East Indian students in the Netherlands from 1946 until 1950 and taught theology in the seminary of the Church of East Java in Indonesia from 1950 until 1954. From 1955 until 1960, he was minister at Knijpe in the Netherlands and, from 1960 until 1971, he was the director of 'Kerk en Wereld' at Driebergen. Since 1971, he has been teaching theology at Nijmegen.

KNUD LØGSTRUP was born in Copenhagen in 1905. After completing his theological studies he served for a period as pastor of a parish, before being appointed in 1943 to the Chair of Ethics and Philosophy of Religion in the University of Århus, a post which he held for thirty-two years. He is an honorary doctor of the Universities of Lund and Marburg. His publications include books on Kierkegaard, Heidegger and Kant.

JOHANN BAPTIST METZ was born in 1928 in Welluck, near Auerbach in Bavaria. He was ordained priest in 1954. He is Professor of Fundamental Theology in the University of Münster and a member of the commission appointed to establish the University of Bielefeld. His publications include *Christliche Anthropozentrik* (Munich 1962); *Kirche im Prozess der Aufklärung* (1970); *Die Theologie in der interdisziplinären Forschung* (1971); *Unsere Hoffnung* (1975); *Zeit der Orden? Zur Mystik und Politik der Nachfolge* (1977, 3rd ed. 1978); *Glaube in Geschichte und Gesellschaft* (1977, 2nd ed. 1978).

THEO SALEMINK was born in 1946 and studied theology at the Catholic University of Nijmegen. His doctor's thesis on Christianity and power, an analysis of the 1971 synod of bishops, was published in 1972. Since 1974, he has taught Church and social history at the centre for agogic and theological education at Utrecht and since 1972 he has also edited *Eltheto,* a journal for religion and politics. His publications include articles in this journal, especially No. 53 (1976), pp. 6-22, and he has edited *Marxisten over Godsdienst* 1844-1914 (Zeist 1978).

DIETER SCHELLONG was born in Kiel in 1928. He studied theology and music at the Universities of Münster, Göttingen and Basle, and became a pastor in Gütersloh in 1956. He became ordinarius Professor for Protestant Theology and Religious Instruction at the Gesamthochschule in Paderborn in 1972. His most important publications (apart from those mentioned in the footnotes) are as follows: *Calvins Auslegung der synoptischen Evangelien* (München 1969) and, 'Theologie nach 1914' in the *Festschrift for Helmut Gollwitzer*.

NORBERT SCHIFFERS was born in 1927 and is Professor of Religious Studies at Regensburg University, West Germany. Among his most recent books are the following: *Befreiung zur Freiheit; Gefangene; Theorie der Religion*. Among fifty-two articles that have appeared in philosophical and theological journals are contributions to *Revista Eclesiastica Brasileira* (December 1976) and *Ciências Humanas* (March 1977). He is an honorary member of the Sociedade Brasileira de Filosofos Catolicos.

WOLFGANG STEGEMANN was born in 1945. He studied Protestant theology in Heidelberg 1968-1973, and was Assistant Lecturer in New Testament studies, University of Mainz 1973-1977. Since 1977 he has been pastor of a parish near Heidelberg.

ARTHUR WASKOW is Director of the Project on American Jewish Institutions at the Public Resource Center in Washington, DC. He is the author of numerous books such as *Godwrestling* (1978); *The Freedom Seder* (1970); *The Limits of Defense* (1962); *From Race Riot to Sit-in* (1965).